T0215069

Demystifying the Azure Well-Architected Framework

Guiding Principles and Design Best Practices for Azure Workloads

Shijimol Ambi Karthikeyan

Apress®

Demystifying the Azure Well-Architected Framework: Guiding Principles and Design Best Practices for Azure Workloads

Shijimol Ambi Karthikeyan
Bangalore, Karnataka, India

ISBN-13 (pbk): 978-1-4842-7118-6   ISBN-13 (electronic): 978-1-4842-7119-3
https://doi.org/10.1007/978-1-4842-7119-3

Managing Director, Apress Media LLC: Welmoed Spahr
Acquisitions Editor: Smriti Srivastava
Development Editor: Laura Berendson
Coordinating Editor: Shrikant Vishwakarma

Cover designed by eStudioCalamar

Cover image designed by Pexels

Distributed to the book trade worldwide by Springer Science+Business Media LLC, 1 New York Plaza, Suite 4600, New York, NY 10004. Phone 1-800-SPRINGER, fax (201) 348-4505, e-mail orders-ny@springer-sbm.com, or visit www.springeronline.com. Apress Media, LLC is a California LLC and the sole member (owner) is Springer Science + Business Media Finance Inc (SSBM Finance Inc). SSBM Finance Inc is a **Delaware** corporation.

For information on translations, please e-mail booktranslations@springernature.com; for reprint, paperback, or audio rights, please e-mail bookpermissions@springernature.com, or visit www.apress.com/rights-permissions.

Apress titles may be purchased in bulk for academic, corporate, or promotional use. eBook versions and licenses are also available for most titles. For more information, reference our Print and eBook Bulk Sales web page at www.apress.com/bulk-sales.

Any source code or other supplementary material referenced by the author in this book is available to readers on GitHub via the book's product page, located at www.apress.com/978-1-4842-7118-6. For more detailed information, please visit www.apress.com/source-code.

Printed on acid-free paper

Dedicated to my dearest Amma and Achan,
my guardian angels watching over me from heaven.

Table of Contents

About the Author ix

About the Technical Reviewer xi

Acknowledgments xiii

Introduction xv

Chapter 1: Azure Well-Architected Framework: What and Why? 1

Digital Transformation Through Azure 2

Why Do You Need a Framework for Architecture Excellence? 3

What Is the Azure Well-Architected Framework? 7

Practical Annotations 10

    Scenario 1 10

    Scenario 2 10

    Scenario 3 11

    Scenario 4 12

Key Takeaways 13

Chapter 2: Cost Optimization: Return on Your Cloud Investment 15

How to Design for Optimal ROI 15

    Design Principles 16

    Design Process 21

    Tools and Services for Cost Optimization 26

Understand the Trade-Offs 36

Configure Reports for Visibility 37

Key Takeaways 38

Chapter 3: Operational Excellence: Keep the Lights On 39

How to Design for Operational Excellence 39

    Design Principles 40

Start with the Application Design 43

Adopt "Everything as Code" 48

Enable Peak Performance for the Deployment Ecosystem 50

Always "Shift Left" for Testing 51

Integrated Monitoring 53

Use Case Analysis 58

    Scenario 3 58

Chapter 4: Performance Efficiency: Meet the Demand Spikes 63

Design Principles for Performance Efficiency 63

    Design Process 67

Make Best Use of Cloud Scalability 71

Identify Bottlenecks Through Performance Testing 74

Monitoring Metrics for Performance 77

Use Case Analysis 79

    Scenario 2 79

Key Takeaways 82

Chapter 5: Reliability: Build Resilient Applications in the Cloud 83

Design Principles for Resiliency 83

Popular Adoption Strategies to Meet the Defined SLAs 86

    Considerations While Defining Application SLAs 87

    Conduct Failure Mode Analysis 88

    Adoption Strategies 93

Testing and Monitoring 95

    Test Strategies 95

    Monitoring and Optimization 97

Use Case Analysis 99

    Scenario 4 99

Key Takeaways 104

Chapter 6: Security: Protect Your Workloads in the Cloud 105

Understanding Threat Vectors in the Cloud 105

Adaptable Security for New-World Threats......................................107

    Design Principles 109

Secure Infrastructure, Data, Network, and Application 114

Identity Is the New Security Perimeter 118

Azure Native Security Tools for Your SOC Team 119

Use Case Analysis 127

    Scenario 1 127

Key Takeaways 130

Index 131

About the Author

Shijimol Ambi Karthikeyan has more than 15 years of experience in data center management, server administration, virtualization, and cloud technologies. She is currently working as a technical delivery manager focusing on Azure infrastructure, automation, DevOps, serverless, and related technologies. She is a tech enthusiast and loves writing about the latest developments in IT infrastructure and cloud computing on her blog at `https://thetechnologychronicle.blogspot.com/`.

About the Technical Reviewer

 **Vikas Sukhija** has more than a decade of IT infrastructure experience with expertise in messaging, collaboration, and IT automations. He is a blogger, architect, and Microsoft MVP, and he is known by the alias TechWizard. As an experienced professional, he assists small to large enterprises in architecting and implementing Office 365 and Azure.

Community contributions from him can be found at the following locations:

Blog: TechWizard.cloud

Facebook: https://www.facebook.com/TechWizard.cloud

Twitter: https://twitter.com/techwizardcloud

Coderepo: https://github.com/VikasSukhija

Acknowledgments

First, I would like to thank my parents for everything I have ever accomplished in my life, including this book. My mother, Ambi R., always inspired me to work toward my goals no matter how unrealistic others perceived them to be. My father, Karthikeyan M., taught me that it is equally important to slow down at times and take in life as it is. They are no longer around, but their love and blessings keep me going.

The last year has been unprecedented and taught us new ways of living our lives during a pandemic. I cannot thank enough my support system, my family and friends, who helped me brave this storm and inspired me to take up the endeavor of writing this book amid multiple challenges. Special shout-out to my daughter, Sanjana Sujai, for inspiring me to be the best version of myself every day. I am thankful to the mentors in my professional life (there are too many to name) for their constant support and encouragement. Last but not least, I would like to thank the entire team at Apress for their support during the publishing process.

Introduction

Cloud-first applications have become the norm rather than the exception in today's cloud-first, mobile-first world. Azure is leading the pack among the cloud platforms in terms of portfolio of services, global coverage, and availability of enterprise adoption frameworks. Azure Well-Architected Framework provides best-practice guidance to customers on how to design, build, operate, and manage the lifecycle of applications in the cloud so as to derive the optimal outcome.

Azure Well-Architected Framework (WAF) is based on five pillars: cost optimization, performance efficiency, operational excellence, reliability, and security. This book will deep dive into these five pillars of WAF and provide practical guidance on adopting them for your Azure workloads. The book starts with an introduction chapter on WAF, its relevance, and an overview of the five encompassing elements. The subsequent chapters will deep dive into each of the WAF pillars in detail. The book also covers some of the common cloud workload use cases and the considerations while adopting WAF for the respective architectures. The concepts are explained in a simple and concise manner that can be comprehended by Azure cloud teams irrespective of their level of expertise.

CHAPTER 1

Azure Well-Architected Framework: What and Why?

With the digital transformation of the modern world, the cloud real estate of organizations has expanded beyond expectation. Be it big data services, analytics, machine learning, or AI, everything has found a home in the cloud. With this transformation, it has become a challenge for architects to choose the best-suited architectures for each of these workloads. There are many aspects to be considered, starting from designing and deploying the applications to keeping the lights on at an optimal cost. Azure, being one of the leading cloud service providers, offers the Azure Well-Architected Framework to support organizations.

The Azure Well-Architected Framework provides definitive guidelines for deploying your workloads in Azure that are aligned with Microsoft-recommended best practices. The framework leverages five architecture elements: cost optimization, performance efficiency, operational excellence, reliability, and security. This book will deep dive into these five elements and provide practical guidance on incorporating them into your

© Shijimol Ambi Karthikeyan 2021
S. Ambi Karthikeyan, *Demystifying the Azure Well-Architected Framework*,
https://doi.org/10.1007/978-1-4842-7119-3_1

architecture. In this first chapter, we will try to understand the relevance of the Well-Architected Framework and why it should form the baseline of all your design decisions while deploying applications in Azure.

Digital Transformation Through Azure

Digital transformation in simple terms means leveraging the latest technologies to revamp how you run your business. The plethora of services available in the cloud has revolutionized this process. Azure is a clear favorite among organizations because it is a trusted partner for digital transformation, irrespective of whether they are Fortune 500 companies or small and medium-sized businesses. Some of the key drivers for the same are listed here:

–   With a global span of 60+ regions and 6,000+ services (at the time of writing this book), Azure offers organizations the flexibility to adopt the cloud the way they want to.

–   Azure has clearly defined hybrid cloud adoption methodologies, which allows organizations to start small and test the waters before taking the plunge.

–   Organizations with existing investments in Windows licenses and technologies prefer Azure as it is an easy extension of their native processes.

–   Azure provides comprehensive coverage for open source technologies: Linux, Kubernetes, Docker, Python, Node.js, HDInsight, TensorFlow, etc., to name a few. This enables innovation and flexibility for cloud adoption through open source frameworks.

- Microsoft has a strong partner ecosystem to onboard your workloads to Azure and support them. Organizations can use the managed service model from Microsoft Cloud Solution Provider (CSP) partners to embark on their digital transformation journey.

- It has an unwavering focus on security, with a dedicated Microsoft Trust Center to guide you on all your security, privacy, and compliance needs.

- It has a robust portfolio of services, with the latest and greatest on AI, data analytics, databases, IOT, serverless, or quantum computing, to name a few. Irrespective of industry vector and business outcomes, there are multiple options to choose from for your digital transformation.

Why Do You Need a Framework for Architecture Excellence?

The reason for a digital transformation is often anchored on a business need; it could be anything from improving the customer experience to expanding the existing service portfolio to a demand for speed and agility to be competitive in the market. A successful digital transformation goes through multiple phases. It starts with mapping out the business requirements, envisioning the end state, and identifying the right platform and technologies, followed by planning and executing the activities.

The Microsoft Cloud Adoption Framework can be leveraged here to arrive at the right strategies and technologies to be used. Though not the focus of this book, the Cloud Adoption Framework complements the Azure Well-Architected Framework. A high-level synopsis of the Cloud Adoption Framework is listed here for context:

1. *Strategy*: In this initial phase, the focus will be on identifying the business outcomes and understanding the motivation for cloud adoption. What are the pain points that you are trying to address through cloud adoption? Which project do you want to prioritize and start with?

2. *Plan*: Once the strategy is finalized, the next step is to create an action plan for adoption. This requires the business stakeholder buy-in, aligning the right people for implementing the adoption plan and enabling them through a readiness plan.

3. *Ready*: This is where you start your cloud journey by creating a landing zone. Note that there will be considerations from the Well-Architected Framework that contributes to this process. The landing zone should be aligned with best practices and ready by the end of this phase to host your initial workloads.

4. *Adopt*: During the Adopt phase, you either migrate or modernize your workloads for the cloud or innovate and develop new solutions to deliver the desired business outcomes. Both approaches require adherences to best-practice guidance and integrating the right pillars from the Well-Architected Framework.

5. *Govern*: This phase involves establishing an initial governance framework for your Azure cloud workloads and improving it iteratively.

6. *Manage*: Define the parameters required for ongoing operations, focusing on business-critical metrics, analyzing workload telemetry, ensuring ongoing compliance, and ensuring business continuity.

While the Cloud Adoption Framework helps to accelerate your digital transformation, the Well-Architected Framework provides prescriptive guidance at a workload level to develop a robust application architecture in the cloud.

Often while focused on the outcome, organizations tend to overlook the nitty-gritty details of having a robust architecture framework to start with. The need for having the right architecture for your applications in the cloud cannot be emphasized enough. It forms the foundation of your digital transformation efforts. The nuances of the architecture vary depending on whether you want to leverage cloud-native services focusing mostly on PaaS/serverless or rather do a lift-and-shift of an existing architecture to the cloud by leveraging IaaS. Irrespective of the approach you choose, a framework for architecture excellence will act as a guiding force to deploy your workloads right the first time.

There are some questions that every architect should ponder while you design and build an application for Azure, and the Well-Architected Framework helps you get the answers right. Let's look at some of the considerations of application architecture that outline the need for such a framework.

- Your application might have an ever-fluctuating performance demand, but the cloud can accommodate all of that if designed right. For example, it is important to decide whether to scale up or scale out. What approach fits best for your workload?

- Continuous monitoring and optimization are also required to maintain the performance levels as the application evolves. You might have started out with one compute instance, but would that be enough to sustain performance as your customer base increases?

- Ensuring operational excellence starts at the application design phase and is not an afterthought. It is closely related to how well DevOps principles are integrated into your application lifecycle. However, are DevOps and CI/CD practices applicable only for application code deployment? How about infrastructure?

- Applications should be designed to be resilient and highly available so as to keep the lights on and the experience consistent for your customers. How robust is your disaster recovery plan? Have you considered the RPO and RTO requirements of your business?

- The security of cloud applications is a work stream in itself, which requires a detailed assessment of possible attack vectors and implementing preventive measures. Have you considered the security of control plane along with the data plane?

- Last but not the least is focus on cost optimization to ensure optimal return on your cloud investments. Though the cloud follows a pay-as-you-go model, it is important to plan for the right sizing and scalability of cloud resources so that you eventually pay only for what you use.

What Is the Azure Well-Architected Framework?

When your workloads are in the cloud, the constructs of deployment, configuration, and operations are strikingly different from what you would have used on-premises. Adopting the right architecture, without doubt, is the key to successfully hosting an application in the cloud. Azure helps you with this every step of the process through the Azure Well-Architected Framework. Consider this as a blueprint for excellence in the Azure cloud. It consists of five main pillars: cost optimization, operational excellence, performance efficiency, reliability, and security.

Here are the concepts covered by the five pillars of the Azure Well-Architected Framework in brief:

- *Cost optimization*: The basic principle is to start small and scale as you go. Instead of making a huge investment up front, it is recommended to follow the approach of Build-Measure-Learn, which is aligned with the Azure Cloud Adoption Framework (CAF). It focuses on building a minimum viable product (MVP), measuring the feedback, and then using a "fail fast" approach to optimize your cost. The Azure Cost Calculator can help you to get the initial cost, and then you can use services like Azure Cost Management to review the ongoing operational cost.

- *Operational excellence*: The success of a cloud deployment depends on how well-oiled your operations engine is. Starting with the automation of deployment to monitoring, logging, and diagnostics, the more granular your visibility is, the better placed you are to keep the lights on for your production environment. The monitoring and logging approach

7

has to be consistent across cloud resources to achieve this goal. The raw monitoring data stored in a central storage can be leveraged by tools like log analytics to get to the root of operational issues, enabling faster resolution. Visualization tools can be leveraged to spot trends such as resource utilization and unusual traffic and alert the operations team.

- *Performance efficiency*: End users expect a solution to perform well irrespective of the traffic being handled by it. One of the main perks of cloud adoption is scaling on demand, which can be vertical scaling or horizontal scaling. Vertical scaling helps you to increase the compute power and capacity of your resources on demand, such as increasing the number of CPU cores when your workloads are in peak demand. Horizontal scaling, on the other hand, is adding more instances of the resources, automatically if possible. Horizontal scaling embodies the true power of cloud-scale deployments and is often cheaper than increasing capacity of a single instance. Additional considerations for performance efficiency include network, storage, and database performance.

- *Reliability*: No matter how airtight the architecture is, the possibility of downtime or a failure is not 100 percent eliminated. Hence, it is important to design your systems to be reliable; in other words, they should be able to recover from failures with minimal damage. Reliability is a combined function of resiliency and availability. Because of the distributed nature of deployments in the cloud, the failure of one component would impact multiple other components. The rule of thumb is to leverage the built-in resiliency features for the native cloud services, be it your VMs, databases, or storage services. Not just your infrastructure layer, but your application logic should also be built on this principle for the solution to be completely reliable.

- *Security*: Security in the cloud is multilayered. You need to consider the infrastructure and network security, application layer security, and data security at rest and in transit. As identity is considered the new security perimeter, selecting and implementing the right identity management solution is the first step in securing your applications. Security of the management plane and data pane should be taken into account here. RBAC leveraging Azure AD takes care of the management plane, by helping you implement fine-grained access control to Azure resources. For a data plane, there are multiple options depending on the Azure service being used, such as data encryption, TDE, etc. In addition to application development security best practices, you can leverage services like application gateways that can provide layer 7 security from common attack vectors.

Figure 1-1 summarizes the focus area of each of the five pillars.

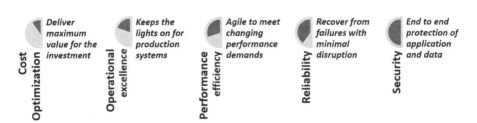

Figure 1-1. *Each pillar will be discussed in detail in subsequent chapters along with practical scenarios and use cases*

Practical Annotations

The success of any framework depends on how easy or how difficult it is to adapt it to real-world scenarios. Given in this section are a few such use cases. We will explore the fit of the Well-Architected Framework for these use cases in upcoming chapters.

Scenario 1

Industry: Health and Life Sciences

With healthcare going digital, there are different options available for consumers such as fitness bands, online consultations, medication tracking, etc. A health and life sciences company can leverage the Well-Architected Framework while developing a cloud-based digital experience for its customers. Here are some key considerations for the scenario:

- There is lot of personally identifiable information (PII) involved, and hence data privacy and security are two of the primary concerns.

- The services should be accessible to customers when they need it and where they need it.

- The response time of applications should ensure a smooth customer experience.

- Adhere to HIPAA controls.

Scenario 2

Industry: Retail

Ecommerce has become a key enabler for the retail industry. It is a highly competitive arena, so customers are spoiled by all the choices. Ecommerce websites should be designed for optimal customer experience to ensure repeatable business. The Azure Well-Architected Framework can help by identifying the right components for hosting, scaling, and securing ecommerce solutions and also to ensure long-term sustainability. Here are some key considerations for the scenario:

- Regular updates of catalogs to cover new product releases

- Secure payment transactions and storage personal information

- Quick retrieval of specific product information and possible alternatives

- Search experience personalized to customer preferences and previous purchases

- Capability to handle peak hour traffic such as Black Friday sales

Scenario 3

Industry: Any

Azure offers multiple managed container solutions, the most popular one being Azure Kubernetes Service (AKS). The service has accelerated the adoption of microservices-based architectures in the cloud. Be it a lift-and-shift of existing containers from on-premises or a modernization of existing applications for the cloud, AKS is leading the way, and this approach is popular across almost all industry vectors. Here are some key considerations while integrating the Well-Architected Framework for microservices-based architectures:

- Persistent data storage and availability

- Scalability consideration (pods in the deployment versus nodes in the cluster)

- Ongoing operational hygiene of the deployment

- Resilience and recovery from failures

- Health telemetry, analytics, and continuous optimization

- Secure access (ingress, communication between microservices, access to application keys, etc.)

Scenario 4

Industry: Financial

Most financial-sector organizations such as banks and insurance companies are faced with challenges of adapting their legacy systems to cloud. There could be some hard dependencies, but most of them can be circumvented by leveraging the right pillars of the Well-Architected Framework. Here are some key considerations of using the Well-Architected Framework while migrating financial-sector line-of-business (LOB) applications to Azure:

- Identity integration for seamless experience, for both customers and employees

- Resiliency of workloads migrated to Azure; downtimes can be unacceptable for banking solutions

- Leveraging PaaS services for modernizing some of the legacy components

- Security of data at rest after migration and in transit during migration

- Flexibility to adopt hybrid architectures; some components might still remain on-premises due to security/compliance reasons

- Visibility into security posture of the environment post migration, identifying malicious activities, and doing proactive remediation

Key Takeaways

The success of a digital transformation lies in setting the context early on and identifying the best-fit tools, services, and framework for implementation. In this chapter, we explored the need for the Well-Architected Framework to enable digital transformation. The five pillars of the Well-Architected Framework were also introduced and how they fit into your cloud adoption strategy. With the Azure Well-Architected Framework, most of the work is etched out for you, and diligence applied in adapting it will make your cloud adoption more efficient. In subsequent chapters, we will be exploring the five pillars of the Well-Architected Framework in detail. We will also correlate them to some real-world adoption scenarios that will help you better understand the concepts.

CHAPTER 2

Cost Optimization: Return on Your Cloud Investment

With an increase in cloud real estate, resource sprawl can become a reality if environments are not managed effectively. Though converting capex to opex is one of the major advantages of cloud computing, you should have a laser focus on optimizing your cloud costs before you even deploy the first resource to ensure the optimal return on investment (ROI). It is a misnomer that monitoring your cloud usage will help with optimizing the cost; it is only one aspect of the solution. In this chapter, we will explore the considerations for cost optimization while deploying your workloads to Azure.

How to Design for Optimal ROI

Designing for optimal ROI is a continuous process, as you will have to revisit it throughout the application lifecycle. Cost optimization can be pivoted on the design principles covered next.

Design Principles

Here are the design principles.

1. **Identify the right costing model.**

    Azure provides a pay-as-you-go model, but there are
    different flavors that you can choose from. Along with
    the compute charges, the software cost, the OS cost,
    etc., are included in the pricing. You also have options
    to reuse your existing on-premises licenses using
    BYOL options. This is applicable for Microsoft software
    as well as for third-party appliances that you want to
    add to the architecture. Consider the following options
    for reducing the cost as you design the environment:

    –   *Azure hybrid benefit*: Customers with existing
        Windows Server, SQL licenses, Red Hat, or SUSE
        Linux subscriptions can use the same licenses in
        Azure to reduce cost.

    –   *Azure spot virtual machines*: If your workloads can
        be interrupted and resumed, then Azure spot VMs
        can be used to get up to 90 percent discount. They
        leverage unused compute capacity in Azure. You
        agree on a maximum price you are willing to pay
        and the VMs are evicted if Azure does not have
        compute capacity or if the cost of the VM is higher
        than the agreed price.

    –   *Reservations*: With Azure reserved instances,
        you can reserve Windows or Linux VMs up front
        for a period of one year or three years to get an
        additional discount on pay-as-you-go prices.
        This can be combined with hybrid to get an up to

80 percent discount on the overall cost. There is a flexibility to pay the cost up front or on a monthly basis. However, if you reserve the instances and choose to cancel before the agreed time frame, there is an early termination fee involved.

– *Azure dev/test pricing*: For nonproduction dev/ test environments, customers can benefit from the special dev/test pricing provided by Azure. There are different options for the same thing: Azure monthly credit for Visual Studio subscribers, enterprise dev/test agreements or pay-as-you-go dev/test subscriptions with reduced rates for a specific set of Azure services such as VMs, cloud services, SQL databases, Logic App, App Services, and HD Insight.

2. **Choose the right size of resources for the business case.**

Finding the right resource for your architecture and right sizing the resource plays an important role in keeping the costs at a minimum. You need to look at the required compute capability, storage capacity, traffic, or transaction requirements while selecting the resource. Another decision point is the level of control you want over the resources. For example, if you want control over the end-to-end application stack, you might want to use IaaS resources instead of PaaS services. Even with IaaS, you will have to drill down on the identified components. For example, are you choosing the right VM and disk SKUs?

The redundancy options should also be considered while selecting the resources. For example, storage services by default would provide three copies of your data in the same region by default, i.e., locally redundant storage. You can go with georedundant storage (GRS) to get three copies of the data in a paired region. However, this would incur more than double the cost of LRS. For your dev-test environments, you might want to stick with LRS, while production workloads can use GRS, but only if they need georedundancy.

With each resource type, be aware of the different billing meters associated with it. For example, the cost of a storage account is not just for the capacity; it also includes the cost of read/write operations, listing and creating container operations, data write and retrieval operations, etc. Often customers get blindsided by the primary cost meter (capacity in the case of storage) and do not take the other billing meters into consideration.

Overprovisioning is one of the most common reason for increased cloud cost. Customers prefer to be cautious and start with the larger SKU than actually required by the application. For example, a low transaction database may not actually need premium disks, which could eat away at your monthly cloud budget. The recommended approach is to start small, monitor usage, and then adjust the SKU size if you hit any bottlenecks.

3. **Keep the budget in sight.**

    The design decisions are pivoted on the requirements of applications; however, the cost aspects of the application components should also be considered

in the decision-making process. Always keep the
budget in sight and explore the cost implications of
design decisions. The application should adhere to the
desired levels of high availability, resiliency, scalability,
security, etc. However, while creating the architecture
pattern, make sure you are not over-engineering the
solution.

For example, consider multiregion deployment
patterns that help protect the application from
regional disasters. However, running an active-active
deployment for DR would be more costly than an
active-passive deployment. If the RPO/RTO permits,
you can go for an active-passive approach where the
resources can be redeployed in the target region in
the event of a disaster through predefined and tested
DevOps processes. For applications that cannot afford
downtime, this may not be a possibility, and an active-
active DR pattern would be required. In such cases,
cost optimization can be done as well by running a
scaled-down version of a DR environment, which can
then be scaled up in the event of a failover.

4. **Plan for scaling.**

Scalability on demand is one of the key selling
points of the cloud, and you can use it for your
advantage to reduce your monthly cloud bill.
Scaling can be either vertical or horizontal, and this
is one of the architecture pattern decisions.

In a vertical scaling or scale-up approach, you add
capacity to existing resources, such as updating
the VM to a higher SKU to accommodate a spike in

application usage. With the Azure SQL database, you can do dynamic scaling by changing the DTU service tiers or changing the vCore type.

Horizontal scaling, on the other hand, is adding instances to handle the workload. This works best with autoscaling. Identify the right set of metrics that will help you trigger the scaling such as a spike in CPU/memory/IOPS usage in VMs that can trigger the autoscaling of VMs in a VMSS. With Azure SQL databases, you can achieve this using elastic pools. Similarly, autoscaling capabilities are available for services such as Service Fabric, Azure App service, Azure Functions, etc.

Tying scalability back to cost optimization, it can be summarized as follows: allocate only the resources required for your applications at any given point in time so that you pay only for what you are using.

5. **Implement continuous monitoring.**

As mentioned earlier, cost optimization is a continuous process. You cannot just deploy the environment aligned with best practices for cost optimization and forget about it. Applications change, architectures evolve over time, and new components get added. Hence, it is important to do a periodic check of the cost incurred by deployments and do course correction. Monitor the metrics of resources regularly to look for indicators of potential spikes in cost. For example, if your user base has increased over the year, the storage cost would also increase in due time. Hence, you might want to consider tiering unused data to a cheaper tier such as cold storage or an archive to keep the cost in check.

For a detailed analysis of the cost, tagging of resources to the owner of systems would help. For example, tag all Azure resources used by the finance department using the same key-value pair so that you can get a cumulative report of the cost incurred by department in your monthly bill. You can also create cost management alerts based on Azure Resource Consumption. You can generate alerts based on predefined budgets, based on Azure prepayment (for enterprise agreements), or even based on spending quotas defined per department in the enterprise agreement portal.

Design Process

Let's revisit the case study that was introduced in Chapter 1 for retail customers. While the listed key requirements should be met, the cost of the solution should also be managed throughout the entire lifecycle.

Scenario 2

Industry: Retail

Ecommerce has become a key enabler for the retail industry. It is a highly competitive arena, so customers are spoiled by all the choices. Ecommerce websites should be designed for optimal customer experience to ensure repeatable business. The Azure Well-Architected Framework can help by identifying the right components for hosting, scaling, and securing ecommerce solutions and also to ensure long-term sustainability. Here are some key considerations for the scenario:

21

- Regular updates of catalogs to cover new product releases

- Secure payment transactions and storage personal information

- Quick retrieval of specific product information and possible alternatives

- Search experience personalized to customer preferences and previous purchases

- Capability to handle peak hour traffic such as Black Friday sales

Table 2-1 lists some of the key considerations for cost optimization while finalizing the architecture pattern for this use case.

Table 2-1. *Architecture Considerations*

Consideration	Rationale
Where does the customer plan to deploy the solution?	The cost of resources varies across Azure regions.
Will there be any cross-zonal traffic from components in other regions?	If there will be cross-zonal traffic network, ingress/egress traffic cost should be factored in.
Is multiregion deployment required?	This depends on whether the ecommerce website caters to a customer base in only one geography. Or would it be a site catering to customers across the globe?

(continued)

Table 2-1. (*continued*)

Consideration	Rationale
If multiregion is being considered, what is the capacity required per region?	Understand the user base per geography and plan accordingly. A full-scale deployment may not be required in regions with minimal customer base, or you could even redirect the traffic to the closest geography.
Does the solution need multifactor authentication or conditional access?	An additional license cost for Azure AD should be factored in based on the requirement.
Is a DDoS standard enabled?	As ecommerce websites can easily be targeted for DDoS attacks, you might want to enable a DDoS standard, which would incur additional cost depending on the number of resources.
What is the Internet edge security solution?	This depends on whether you are planning to use Azure Firewall, Azure Application Gateway, or third-party edge solutions. If there is an existing investment in a third-party solution with a BYOL option in the cloud, that could bring down the overall cost.
What are the scaling requirements?	The ecommerce application is expected to have spike in usage during holiday and sales seasons. Autoscaling of components can be used here to meet the varying demands and also keep the cost in check.
What are the different environments required for the application?	If there are multiple dev/test environments, use Azure dev/test subscription benefits to reduce cost.

(*continued*)

Table 2-1. (*continued*)

Consideration	Rationale
What are the services being planned for the intelligent search functionality of the ecommerce website?	If an Azure cognitive search solution is being used, estimate the capacity requirements before selecting the pricing tier as it cannot be changed later.
Is a CDN being considered to enhance user experience?	Identify the zone for CDN and estimate the data transfer rates, and choose between standard and premium flavors of the service.
Deployment model for services such as IaaS/PaaS	Weigh the pros and cons of deploying application and databases in VMs versus leveraging services such as Azure App Service or Azure SQL DB. For example, IaaS gives more control over the stack but would incur additional overhead for maintenance, patching, etc., and hence there is an indirect manpower cost involved. Add in a hybrid benefit to the pricing model if you have BYOL options available for the components to calculate the final cost.
What is the expected lifespan of the application?	Understand how the application aligns with the business strategy of the company. Is it part of its long-term digital transformation plan or a short-term plan or stop-gap solution? If it's the former, consider Azure Reservation with an up-front commitment of one year or three years.

(*continued*)

Table 2-1. (*continued*)

Consideration	Rationale
Have you considered the cost differentiating options between production and nonproduction environments for the application?	Avoid falling into the trap of overprovisioning by maintaining all lower environments at the same level as production. Use lower-resource SKUs in nonproduction environments. You can also do away with the high-availability configurations that would need additional resources.
Have you finalized the budget and identified the stakeholders if internal cross charging is required?	Create alerts based on the budget for the ongoing monitoring of cost. Add tags to resources mapping to internal departments for cross charging.
Have you defined the plan for ongoing governance and monitoring of cost?	Cadence should be set for reviewing information from tools like Azure Cost Management or Azure Advisor to further optimize the cost. During the lifecycle of the application, some resources might get replaced, and they should be deleted in time to avoid additional charges. Examples are cost of unused storage, orphaned disks, etc. Additionally, Azure policies can be used to prevent the deployment of resources that do not adhere with the decided SKU, location, features, etc.
Is the application lifecycle management automated?	Ensure the integration of DevOps practices for the agility of the application. This also helps in the quick deployment and deletion of test and development environments on an on-demand basis.
What is the DR strategy for the application?	Depending on the choice between active-active or active-passive, factor in the cost of backup services or cost of additional components in the DR region.

Figure 2-1 summarizes the different phases in the cost optimization process.

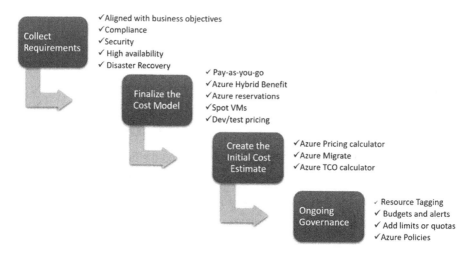

Figure 2-1. *Cost optimization process*

Tools and Services for Cost Optimization

Getting into the practical nuances of cost optimization, let's consider some of the tools that you can use for initial estimation and also for the ongoing monitoring.

Estimation Tools

TCO Calculator: Migrating to the cloud is part of an organization's digital transformation journey and is often an irreversible decision. Along with mapping the right services to host the applications, you would also want to understand the TCO in the long term while migrating workloads from on-premises to Azure. The Azure TCO Calculator is a tool that can be used for this calculation. You can add details of your on-premises workloads, i.e., details of servers, databases, storage, and networking. You can then adjust the default assumptions made by the calculator. For example, adjust your storage redundancy requirement or update your software assurance coverage. The tool is available at `https://azure.microsoft.com/en-us/pricing/tco/calculator/`.

Here I'm showing the three-step calculation process for a sample two-tier application. For the purposes of demonstration, we are considering two servers for the app server front end and two servers for the database back end hosted on the VMware platform.

The first step is to define the workloads. Enter the details of the servers, as shown in Figure 2-2.

Figure 2-2. *Server details*

On the same page, provide the details for the storage and networking, as shown in Figure 2-3.

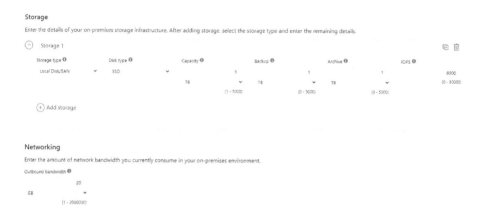

Figure 2-3. *Storage and networking details*

On the next page, adjust the assumptions. In addition to the redundancy and license requirements in Azure, this page also covers other on-premises costs such as hardware, software, electricity, virtualization, etc., which can be adjusted if required, as shown in Figure 2-4.

Software Assurance coverage (provides Azure Hybrid Benefit)

Enable this if you have purchased this benefit for your on-premises Windows or SQL Servers. If enabled, Azure Hybrid Benefit (AHB) will be applied to Azure estimates. AHB helps you get more value from your on-premises licenses — save up to 40 percent on virtual machines and up to 82 percent with Azure Reserved Virtual Machines (VM) instances.

Windows Server Software Assurance coverage

SQL Server Software Assurance coverage

Learn more about Software Assurance >   Learn more about Azure Hybrid Benefit >

Geo-redundant storage (GRS)

GRS replicates your data to a secondary region that is hundreds of miles away form the primary region.

Learn more about GRS >

Virtual Machine costs

Enable this for the Calculator to not recommend Bs-series virtual machines

Learn more about Bs-series virtual machines >

Electricity costs   0.1334   USD

Price per KW hour

Figure 2-4. *Redundancy and license requirements*

In the next step, a report will be generated that projects your TCO and savings. Figure 2-5 and Figure 2-6 show some snippets from the sample report.

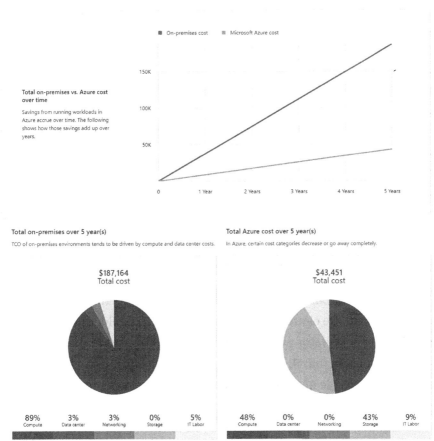

Figure 2-5. *TCO sample report, cost savings over five years*

Figure 2-6. *TCO report, cost breakdown*

Azure Pricing Calculator: If you are deploying greenfield environments in the cloud or migrating brownfield deployments, the Azure Pricing Calculator will come in handy to understand the estimated monthly cost. Note that this will be an estimate, and the actual bill will depend on the usage of the environment. The Azure Pricing Calculator is available at https://azure.microsoft.com/en-us/pricing/calculator/.

The Azure Pricing Calculator helps you understand the cost differences when you use different SKUs, regions, or flavors of the same service. Figure 2-7 shows an example of an estimate for the cost of an app service using Windows OS at the Premium tier.

App Service

| REGION: | | OPERATING SYSTEM: | | TIER: | |
| West US | ⌄ | Windows | ⌄ | Premium V3 | ⌄ ⓘ |

Premium V3

INSTANCE:

P1V3: 2 Cores(s), 8 GB RAM, 250 GB Storage, $0.335 ⌄

| 1 | × | 730 | Hours ⌄ | | = | $244.55 |
| Instances | | | | | | |

Savings Options

Save up to 42% on pay as you go prices with 1 year or 3 year reserved instances

◉ Pay as you go
○ 1 year reserved (~25% discount)
○ 3 year reserved (~40% discount)

$244.55   = $244.55
Average per month   Average per month
($0.00 charged upfront)   ($0.00 charged upfront)

⌄ SSL Connections

| | Upfront cost | $0.00 |
| | Monthly cost | $244.55 |

Figure 2-7. *Azure Pricing Calculator*

If you want to understand the cost difference while hosting the same
SKU in a different region and using a lower SKU for, say, nonproduction
deployments, you can simply update the details in the calculator, as shown
in Figure 2-8.

App Service

| REGION: | | OPERATING SYSTEM: | | TIER: | |
| West US | ⌄ | Windows | ⌄ | Standard | ⌄ ⓘ |

Standard

INSTANCE:

S2: 2 Cores(s), 3.5 GB RAM, 50 GB Storage, $0.200 ⌄

| 1 | × | 730 | hours ⌄ | | = | $146.00 |
| Instances | | | | | | |

⌄ SSL Connections

| | Upfront cost | $0.00 |
| | Monthly cost | $146.00 |

Figure 2-8. *Updating the calculator details*

31

The Azure Pricing Calculator considers all the possible charges while you start using the resource. For example, with storage, it is not just the capacity but the additional charges incurred for the storage read-write operations, container operations, and the data retrieval operations (for cool and archival tiers) that you will be charged for, as shown in Figure 2-9.

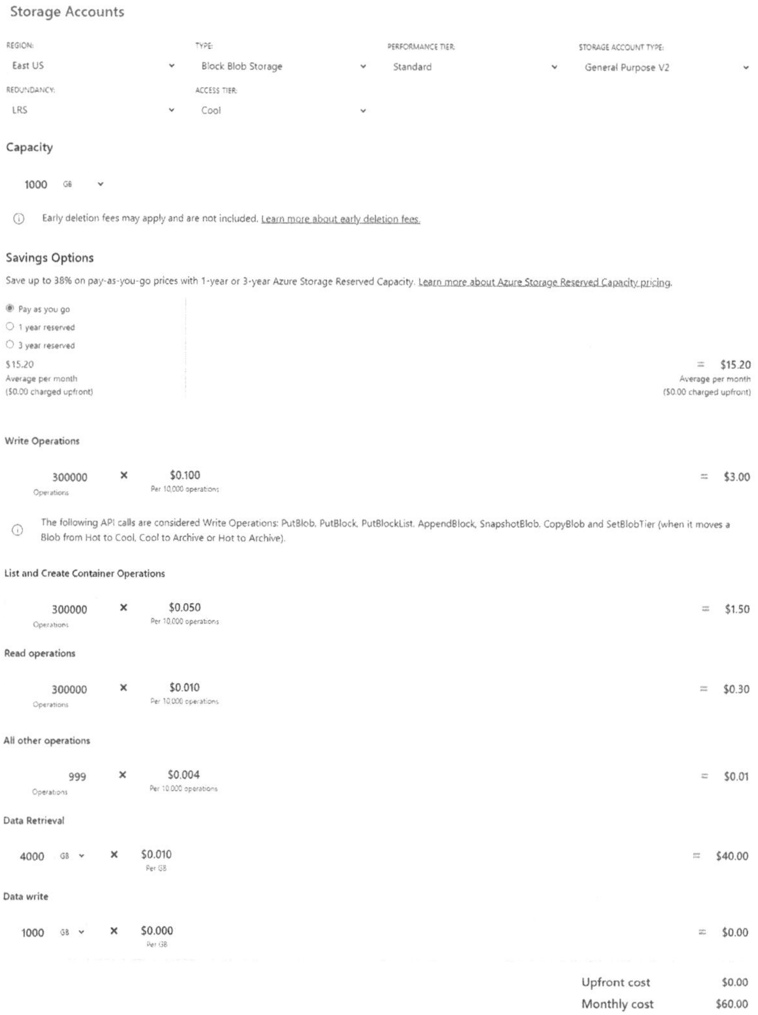

Figure 2-9. *Azure Pricing Calculator, all possible charges*

The estimates created in the Azure Pricing Calculator can be saved or exported for future reference.

Azure Migrate: Azure Migrate is the Microsoft-recommended tool for lift-and-shift migrations to Azure. It can be used to migrate on-premises physical machines, virtual machines hosted in VMware/Hyper-V, or machines hosted in other cloud platforms like AWS or GCP. In addition to providing a unified platform for migration, the tools also provide a cost estimation for the migrated workloads during the assess phase. Here you choose the VM SKUs and apply any discount percent or EA subscription discount or hybrid benefit discounts. Once the assessment is completed, you will get a monthly cost estimate for compute and storage after migration.

Monitoring

Azure Cloud Cost Management: This service provides visibility into your Azure usage patterns and trends. It also uses advanced analytics to predict the Azure monthly cost based on the usage for the month. Any reservations, hybrid benefit discounts, or negotiated prices are also considered by the service. The details provided by Azure Cloud Cost Management provide visibility into the cloud spend, and the tool helps you drill down to the usage and take the necessary cost control steps.

Figure 2-10 shows a sample cost analysis chart with the actual cost and the forecast cost for a billing period for a pay-as-you-go subscription.

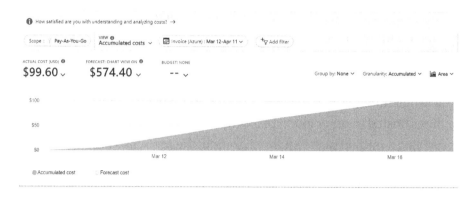

Figure 2-10. *Sample cost analysis chart*

Cost analysis reports on which service/location/resource group name is incurring these charges are also provided, as shown in Figure 2-11. The view can be further customized to get additional views based on resource, tags, reservation name, service tier, and so on.

Figure 2-11. *Cost analysis reports*

Budgets in the cost management service help to define budgets for usage and generate alerts when the cost exceeds the defined limits. Note that budgets and alerts do not stop any of your Azure resources or stop the consumption, but rather help in creating awareness and accountability in your organization about cloud spend.

Azure Advisor: Azure Advisor evaluates your Azure environments and provides cost optimization recommendations. It provides recommendations for the following:

– Right sizing of VMs based on utilization trends

– Shutting down unused VMs based on usage information

– Updating SKU of databases like MariaDB, MySQL, or PostgreSQL if the resources have been under-utilized

– Monitoring and removing unprovisioned ExpressRoute circuits

– Identifying unused virtual network gateways and reducing the cost by deleting or reconfiguring them

– Enumerating resource usage and providing recommendations for reducing cost through reserved instances

– Deleting unused resources that could incur cost, such as IP address, managed disk snapshot, failed data factory pipelines, etc.

Figure 2-12 shows a cost optimization recommendation from Azure Advisor.

Figure 2-12. *Cost optimization recommendation*

Governance Using Azure Policies

Azure policies can be used to enforce governance on the type of resources, location, SKU types, etc. You can use either built-in policies or custom-built policies to suit your business requirements. For example, you can use a built-in policy to restrict the type of resources that cannot be deployed in your environment. This would help in preventing resource sprawl as well as eliminate associated cost.

Understand the Trade-Offs

While making design decisions, there could be trade-offs between the final value proposition and the cost. Often the cost optimization would be pitted against the other four pillars of the Well-Architected Framework.

> *Reliability*: Consider the decision to use multiregion or multizone deployment for the reliability of application. This could mean additional components and additional cost. However, for production deployments, this could be non-negotiable as you need to meet your defined SLAs, RPO, and RTO. You need to carefully evaluate the options and choose lower-cost reliability options such as restoring from backup if the downtime is acceptable.
>
> *Performance efficiency*: Adding additional capacity or using high SKUs for high performance would lead to an increase in the cost. Avoid the trap of overprovisioning—always start with the optimal size and then scale as required. Choose the Azure location where the costs of resources are less, but do not greatly impact the user experience due to access

latencies. When using options like spot VMs, though the price is less, be mindful that the services could be interrupted any time when they get evicted. Use such options only for services that are OK to be interrupted.

Security: Adding additional security components would increase the overall cost of the deployment. Security is non-negotiable, and it is often a trade-off that all organizations would end up accepting in their fold. However, you should be aware of overdoing security. For example, avoid piling up security services in the architecture that essential provide the same functionality.

Operational excellence: There are operational processes that are required to keep the lights on in your Azure environment; however, the investment into them could drive up the cloud cost initially. Examples are the time and effort required to set up automated operations, i.e., manpower, cost of tools, etc. However, over time, the investment would pay off and would eventually help to reduce the cost by avoiding human errors, configuration mistakes, quick rollouts/rollbacks, etc.

Configure Reports for Visibility

Tools like Azure Cost Management and Azure Advisor provides visibility into your Azure cloud cost. You can use Azure consumption APIs to create custom reports for both native and marketplace resources. In addition to out-of-the-box monitoring capabilities provided by Azure Advisor, customers can also create custom scripts using Azure APIs to identify unused or orphaned resources. Azure Cost Management Connector for Power BI Desktop can be used to create customized reports for granular analysis of Azure usage. This service is available for customers having a Microsoft customer agreement or enterprise agreement for Azure.

Key Takeaways

Cost optimization for Azure should be based on the principles of build-measure-learn, where the focus is not on building the perfect solution on day 1, but rather on optimizing as you go. It is greatly dependent on the components and the architecture patterns. However, careful planning of budgets, evaluation of trade-offs, and ongoing monitoring can help in achieving the right balance between cost optimization and the other pillars of the Well-Architected Framework. In the next chapter of this book, we will explore another pillar of WAF, i.e., operational excellence, that will help keep the lights on for your Azure deployments.

CHAPTER 3

Operational Excellence: Keep the Lights On

Operational excellence for any application is based on how to code and ship the application and then manage its lifecycle. Deploying or migrating applications to the cloud is not the end of the journey; what is more important is how you keep the lights on and how efficiently you can do that. This chapter will focus on framework, practices, and processes to be followed to ensure that applications run without disruption. It will cover end-to-end processes starting from the design, deployment, and ongoing monitoring.

How to Design for Operational Excellence

Traditional methodologies of application development and deployment have to give way to DevOps-focused delivery if we want to achieve optimal operational excellence. Let's explore some of the key design principles that will help you achieve this.

© Shijimol Ambi Karthikeyan 2021
S. Ambi Karthikeyan, *Demystifying the Azure Well-Architected Framework*,
https://doi.org/10.1007/978-1-4842-7119-3_3

Design Principles

These are the principles:

1. **Adopt DevOps.**

   The siloed approach where developers and the operations team work independently does not fit well in a cloud-first world, which demands agility and more frequent deployment cycles. Organizations should focus on developing a DevOps model, which is more often a cultural shift. The demarcation between developers and the operations team is no longer there, and everyone is equally accountable for a successful deployment. The DevOps DORA metrics can be used as a quantitative method for measuring your DevOps maturity.

   - *Deployment frequency (DF)*: This metric indicates how often you deploy code to product environments so that your users can benefit from new features/updates/bug fixes, etc. A high level of maturity on this metric would mean that your team can comfortably deploy code as and when required, even if that means multiple deployments in a day.

   - *Mean lead time for changes (MLT)*: This metric measures the time it takes for code committed by a developer to be successfully deployed in a production system. At high levels of efficiency, this should be ideally less than one day.

- *Mean time to recover (MTTR)*: This metric indicates how your DevOps process can handle downtime, which could be due to defects, unplanned outages, etc. It measures the time taken for your application to be back online after such an incident happens. At high levels of efficiency, this should ideally be less than an hour.

- *Change failure rate (CFR)*: This metric indicates the percentage of deployments to production that could lead to downtime or degraded functionality of an application. In other words, it would also indicate the number of deployments calling for an immediate hotfix/rollback/patches, etc. The metrics can be in the range of 0 to 15 percent as a general standard, but the actual value would depend on your application criticality.

2. **Streamline the build and release of workloads.**

   Though it is included as part of DevOps, the process of build and release requires a special callout. Along with application deployment, deploying the underlying infrastructure through IAC ensures that the lifecycle of all application components is streamlined. No different teams or processes are required to handle the infrastructure and your applications separately. The same repeatable process can be used to manage both.

3. **Focus on monitoring and continuous improvement.**

   Monitoring the entire application and infrastructure stack as well as the efficiency of the build and release process can give you key insights into the overall system's operational health. The insights derived from operations telemetry and the DevOps metrics should be fed back into the system to enable continuous improvement. There should be a well-defined process for this, so as to ensure consistency. The outcomes should be measurable as they indicate the improvement in efficiency of your systems over time.

4.   **Design loosely coupled applications.**

With cloud adoption on the rise, complex monolithic applications have given way to loosely coupled architectures. These architectures focus on loosely coupled cloud-native services such as microservices, PaaS, serverless, etc. This approach helps in achieving much better operational excellence when compared to monolithic deployments. The different application components can be managed independently from each other for development, testing, and deployment.

5.   **Learn from failures and incidents.**

Despite best efforts, incidents and failures do happen. Ensure that you have a well-defined incident management process in place and a frontline team available as first responders. Frameworks such as ITIL can be leveraged here as appropriate. Most importantly, aligning with the principle of continuous integration, ensure that there is a process in place to assimilate the lessons learned from such failures.

Start with the Application Design

Release engineering for application design focuses on the easy design and deployment of applications, i.e., the process of actually making the features available for users. This includes but is not limited to the development environments to be used, source control and branching strategies, continuous integration for the code, testing and release management, etc., to name a few. The process should ideally be defined before you even identify the target environment for your deployment.

The first consideration is development environment. The developers should have a fully enabled and integrated environment available to develop and test the code. Be mindful that the code being developed for one component would already have dependency with that of other components or with existing code. With microservices architecture taking a front seat, you might need access to Docker-based development environments. Standing up Kubernetes clusters for each developer is not a practical solution; hence, you can opt for Docker Desktop or the dev clusters of Kubernetes/AKS. Customers can also use the Bridge to Kubernetes solution, which will help you run the code locally on one microservice, with connectivity to the Kubernetes cluster where the rest of your dependent microservices are deployed. The Bridge to Kubernetes solution can be integrated with popular development tools like Visual Studio Code and Visual Studio.

The overall process that will help you enable operational excellence in the application lifecycle can be summarized under five controls, as listed in Figure 3-1. They are source control, continuous integration, test strategy, release performance, and deployment and rollback.

Figure 3-1. *Five controls of operational excellence*

While designing the application lifecycle, each of these controls has to be well defined. Each of them warrants a detailed discussion and decision-making process before you can zero in on an approach or decision. Some of them could even change in the course of the application lifecycle as the business evolves. For example, you could shift from a canary release model to a blue-green deployment approach as the solution matures. The DevOps principles of continuous improvement becomes applicable here directly or indirectly.

The major features that you should take into account for all five controls are summarized here for practical and easy consumption:

1. **Source control management**

   The first step in the development process is checking in the code to a source control management solution of your choice. Figure 3-2 shows some of the features to look for in a source control management tool. Popular options that can be used here include but are not limited to Git, GitHub, Azure Repos, etc.

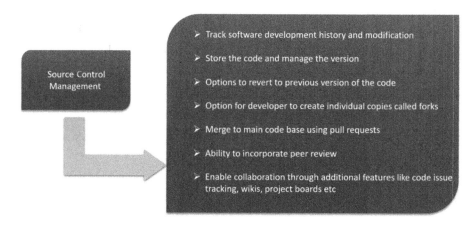

Figure 3-2. Source control management

2. Continuous integration

In enterprise-scale deliveries, there will be a large team of developers working on different application features in parallel. The continuous integration process helps to bring together the code and ensure due diligence so that no breaking changes are introduced into the production systems. Figure 3-3 shows some of the non-negotiable factors of continuous integration.

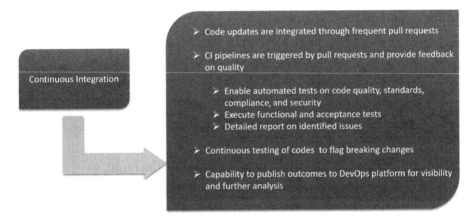

Figure 3-3. *Continuous integration*

3. Test strategy

The scope of testing in an application lifecycle is not limited to continuous integration. The testing strategy should provide end-to-end coverage for your application and infrastructure, as shown in Figure 3-4.

45

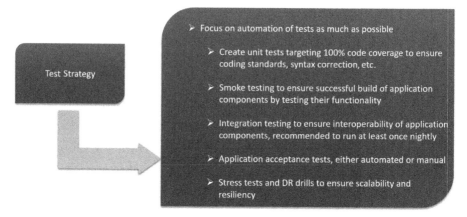

Figure 3-4. *Test strategy*

4. **Release performance**

A successful build indicates that your code is ready
to go. A robust build and release process is a crucial
part of your continuous delivery system. The time
taken to resolve an identified issue will increase if
the code takes a longer time to complete the build.
Hence, it is essential to ensure the performance
of the underlying systems to establish faster
release cycles. Figure 3-5 shows some of the main
considerations.

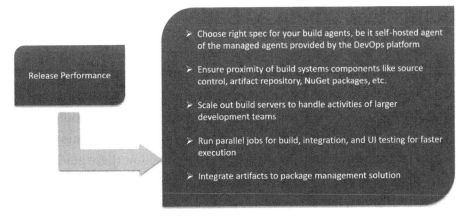

Figure 3-5. *Release performance*

5. **Deployment and rollback**

    Automated deployments and rollbacks help to ensure
    a predictable process for rolling out new updates as
    well as reverting them to a known good state in case of
    errors. Though it's the last-mile process in the software
    lifecycle, careful consideration should be applied while
    defining and executing them. Figure 3-6 shows the
    main considerations for deployment and rollback.

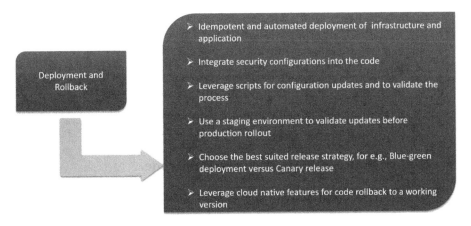

Figure 3-6. *Deployment and rollback*

Adopt "Everything as Code"

To achieve operational excellence, you should consider an "everything as code" approach. That means it's not just the application code that is the focal point; it is also the infrastructure, app configurations, security, etc. Managing them as code helps to avoid untracked changes that could lead to downtime. A known good state is available not just for application code but also for the underlying infrastructure. You can follow these guidelines to firm up the approach for your environment, all the while without compromising on quality:

1. **Ensure code quality for IAC.**

   Just like quality gates implemented for code, enable peer reviews and quality checks for your IAC updates. This will help to ensure that configuration changes being made are aligned with the prescribed best practices. You can also use automated code quality testing frameworks to identify potential issues before the code is deployed to production.

2. **Break silos for infrastructure deployment and updates.**

   With infrastructure being managed as code, you can ensure consistency of the process. This also eliminates dependency on one specific team to configure and deploy and configure new environments. Anyone can leverage the defined automation process for an error-free deployment.

3. **Integrate continuous security in the code.**

   Unlike traditional deployments, security cannot be an afterthought in the cloud. You should start integrating security best practices from day 1. There are many out-of-the-box tools that get integrated into the application code pipelines to ensure security. The same approach is applicable for IAC as well, to ensure that all relevant security best practices and guidelines are taken into account. It goes beyond the typical testing that finds errors in the code. You need to go one layer deeper to analyze the environment configuration that will be created by the code and look for possible security loopholes, such as VMs deployed with permissive NSGs.

4. **Look out for configuration drifts.**

    With IAC, it is the first deployment that creates the environment, and any updates are managed by subsequent deployments. If there is no change in configuration, the redeployment does not have any impact on the environment. Even if there are no changes, you should ensure that the code is redeployed as a prerequisite for your application code, preferably in the same pipeline. This will ensure that no infrastructure-related dependencies are missed in the process. IAC helps in bringing back your resources to a desired state even if any out-of-band manual changes are done in the environment.

5. **Ensure consistency across environments.**

    An enterprise line-of-business application passes through many environments in its lifecycle such as dev, test, QA, prod, hotfix, etc. IAC helps to maintain the same baseline across these production and nonproduction environments, which is not practically possible with a manual approach. Any variations required between the environments can be achieved by adjusting the input variable during deployment. IAC also helps with the scalability of the deployment, where the same code can be used to spin up additional resource instances using the same configuration.

Enable Peak Performance for the Deployment Ecosystem

We briefly touched upon this when we talked about application design under release performance. Defining fine-grained process for build and release management does not always ensure a successful delivery engine. This requires a focused effort to ensure that the underlying systems are robust enough to ensure successful builds every time.

- Ensure that you have deployed the build agent in right-sized VMs. Lack of resources in your build machine can result in slower build and release, which in turn impacts the overall efficiency of the process.

- Using managed agents provided by DevOps tools can help you set up the CI/CD pipelines really quickly, as the agent deployment and configuration are managed by the tool. However, if you need additional control over the build environments, you might want to choose self-hosted agents. With Azure DevOps you can use single VM-based self-hosted agents or VMSS-based scale set agents that can be autoscaled when there are more builds to be run. The latter is recommended for scenarios where the development team size is very large with multiple builds and releases happening at the same time.

- The build server, be it managed or self-hosted, should have proximity and access to your code repository and target machines to deploy artifacts. Proximity plays an important role as the transfer of data over the network happens during the build and release process. Any firewalls between your target systems and the DevOps solution should be configured to allow the necessary communication.

- Use parallel job configurations wherever possible to accelerate the velocity. They can be either multiconfiguration builds, deployments, or testing. For builds you could run debug and release configurations as a parallel job. Applications being deployed in multiple regions can be run as parallel jobs.

Always "Shift Left" for Testing

Testing is the safety net for your code before you deploy tests to production systems. It will ensure that the code being pushed to production will not cause any breaking changes. This is applicable for both infrastructure and application code. Note that tests are not done at the tail end, before the deployment. You should adopt a "shift-left" approach, where testing begins early in the development cycle. Tests should be incorporated at various stages to ensure end-to-end coverage. Consider a test-driven development approach for systems with stringent quality requirements, where the test is written before even the code is written.

The following types of tests should be factored in your build and release process to ensure operational excellence:

- *Unit tests for code*: Units tests are used to test the smallest piece of code without dependency on external systems. It could be a syntax check or testing of a single function, method, etc. You could use frameworks like jUnit or SUnit that can be used for implementing unit testing. Note that the same approach should be applied for IAC as well, where the templates can be checked for syntax and best practices for code.

- *Smoke tests*: These tests focus on the functionality of the components independently. It indicates readiness of the code for further testing such as integration/QA testing. Any major issues in functionalities should be caught at the smoke testing stage, before they progress further in the pipeline.

- *Integration tests*: As name indicates, integration testing ensures that the different components of an application can work together as a single unit. It is more extensive than smoke testing and hence more time-consuming. There are different approaches to integration testing, such as big bang, top-down, bottoms-up, sandwich testing, etc. Depending on nature of your application, the right testing methodology can be adapted.

- *UAT*: The user acceptance testing process has a dependency on how the releases are managed. For instance, the safest approach might be to release the application to a target set of customers through a canary release, allowing them to test new functionalities before releasing to the entire customer base. You can also opt for blue-green deployments where the older version is still maintained so that users can still be redirected to it if the newer version of the application is not working as expected.

There are additional tests such as stress test, fault injection tests, and DR tests that can be incorporated based on your business case.

Integrated Monitoring

Monitoring gives you measurable outcomes that you can leverage for continuous improvement of your application lifecycle. Monitoring is not just focused on application metrics. Consider a holistic approach where you monitor applications from the ground up, from the infrastructure and its surrounding ecosystem, as shown in Figure 3-7.

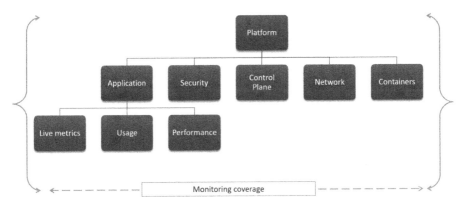

Figure 3-7. Monitoring coverage

Let's explore some of the monitoring tools that will help you implement the right monitoring framework for operational excellence.

Application Insights: This is the flagship tool for application monitoring in Azure with all the key metrics integrated into it out of the box such as resource utilization, dependency mapping, usage analytics, performance, etc. It can be integrated into your application either without any code change or by instrumenting your code to send telemetry data to the tool. You can use release annotations as indicators in Application Insights dashboards, which can help you deep dive into issues that can be correlated back to new releases. Application Insights also provides a live metrics stream view to monitor your application performance in real time. This could help catch any glitches, say during the release process. Figure 3-8 shows a Live Metrics stream from Application Insights.

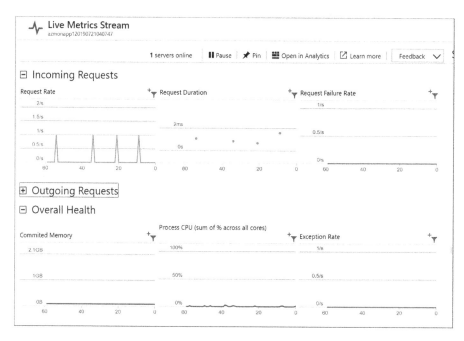

Figure 3-8. *Live Metrics stream from Application Insights*

Azure Monitor: Azure Monitor is the default tool for platform monitoring, and it provides extensive coverage for all Azure services be it VMs, App Services, AKS, network, storage, databases, or any other PaaS services. You can correlate information from Azure Monitor with various components of your application to pinpoint bottlenecks in your environment. There is no additional integration required for Azure Monitor for most of the components as it comes integrated out of the box with metrics relevant for specific services, as shown in Figure 3-9 and Figure 3-10.

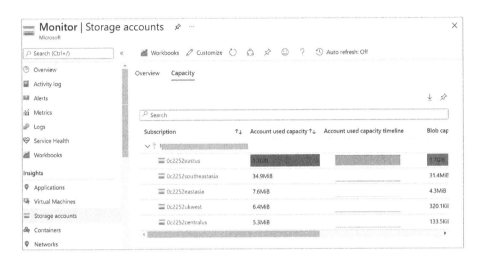

Figure 3-9. *Storage capacity monitoring*

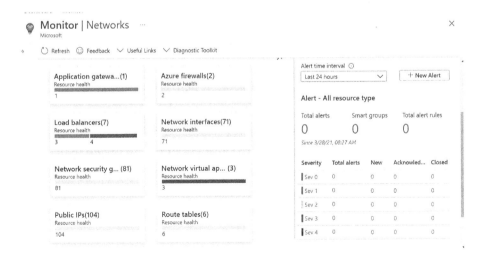

Figure 3-10. *Network resource health*

Container Insights: You can monitor the status of your applications deployed in the Azure Kubernetes service by leveraging Container Insights. It can be used to monitor your AKS cluster nodes, cluster health, and pods running inside the cluster, as shown in Figure 3-11.

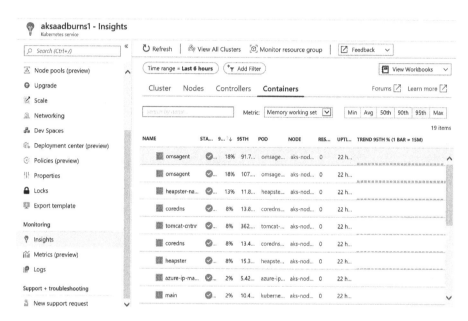

Figure 3-11. *Container Insights*

Activity logs: Azure activity logs give you insights into the control plane activities of your Azure subscription. It helps trace back performance degradations or errors to any control plane events or misconfigurations. The information provided by logs is quite extensive, as shown in Figure 3-12. They can be further integrated with log analytics for further analysis to derive insights. This integration process can be done through IAC pipelines as a best practice.

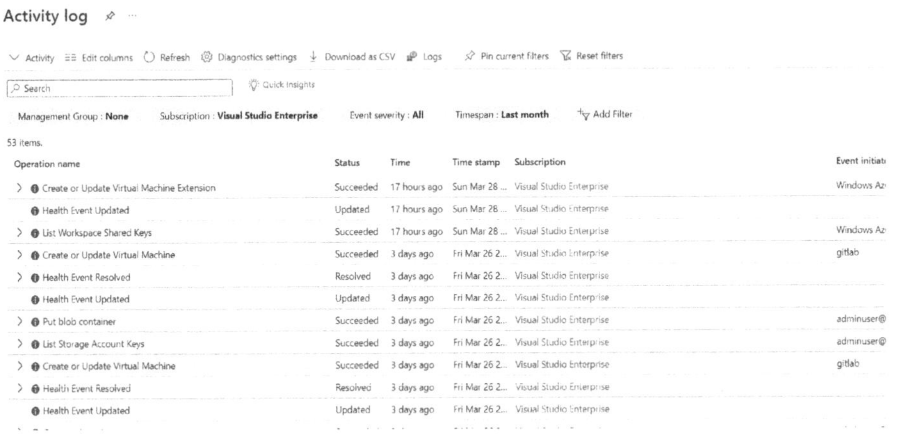

Figure 3-12. *Azure activity logs*

Security Center: Azure Security Center enables cloud security posture management for workloads in Azure. It evaluates environments against security best practices and provides a bird's-eye view on the status of Azure security. The secure score provided by Azure Security Center, as shown in Figure 3-13, enables you to quantify this status. You can leverage the recommendations provided by Azure Security Center to further strengthen your Azure environment's security posture. Note that we will be discussing Azure Security Center in detail in Chapter 6 of this book.

Figure 3-13. *Azure Security Center*

Use Case Analysis

Let's revisit the case study that was introduced in Chapter 1 for container-based deployments. While the listed key requirements should be met, operational excellence should be ensured throughout the entire lifecycle.

Scenario 3

Industry: Any

Azure offers multiple managed container solutions, the most popular one being AKS. The service has accelerated the adoption of microservices-based architectures in the cloud. Be it a lift-and-shift of existing containers from on-premises or modernizing existing applications for the cloud, AKS is leading the way. This approach is popular across almost all industry vectors. Here are some key considerations when integrating the Well-Architected Framework for microservices-based architectures:

- Persistent data storage and availability

- Scalability consideration, pods in the deployment versus nodes in the cluster

- Ongoing operational hygiene of the deployment

- Resilience and recovery from failures

- Health telemetry, analytics, and continuous optimization

- Secure access, ingress, communication between microservices, access to application keys, etc.

Figure 3-14 shows a standard AKS deployment architecture available in Azure Architecture Center for reference. Note that this has to be customized further as per the business requirements of the customer.

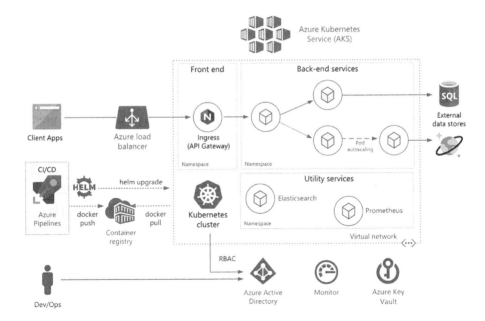

Figure 3-14. *Azure Architecture Center (image courtesy: Azure Architecture Center)*

Table 3-1 summarizes some of the key considerations for operational excellence while finalizing the architecture pattern for this use case.

Table 3-1. *Summary of Operational Excellence*

Consideration	Rationale
What geography does the customer plan to deploy the solution?	Ensure the proximity of the DevOps solution to the target environments and that relevant connectivity requirements are addressed.
Is multiregion deployment required?	In a multiregion cluster deployment of AKS, ensure that the IAC pipelines are designed to deploy the component to both regions.
What are the scaling requirements of pods?	Factor in horizontal pod auto scalar conditions in configuration files checked into the source code repository.
What are the different environments required for the application?	Enable namespace configuration in deployment YAML files if using namespace-based segregation for different environments.
What is the approach for packaging and deploying the application?	Choose between the direct deployment of YAML files or Helm chart-based deployment integrating with the Azure container registry for centralized management.
How are RBAC controls enabled in AKS?	While using Azure AD integrated RBAC, the configuration steps have to be integrated in the deployment pipeline.
Are workload responsibilities distributed between teams?	It's recommended to start with a fundamental framework like a hub-and-spoke network, Azure AD integration, ingress configuration, etc., with responsibilities of different teams clearly defined.

(*continued*)

Table 3-1. (*continued*)

Consideration	Rationale
What is the process for building container images for updating applications?	Ensure that you have a CI process in place to integrate new code into container images that gets deployed to cluster through CD.
How do you ensure the redundancy of container images?	Update the IAC code to deploy a container registry premium SKU if georedundancy is required.
What is the workload/cluster deployment strategy?	Have isolated preproduction and production deployment environments. The deployment pipelines should target preproduction environments first and run extensive tests/validations before changes are pushed to production.
What is the scope of the build pipeline of the application?	This involves getting the application code from source control with the latest updates to build the image/Helm charts that can be pushed to the Azure container registry, and the artifacts get published.
What is the scope of the release pipeline of the application?	Retrieve the artifacts based on the Docker image version and deploy to the target AKS cluster.
How do you integrate monitoring from day 1?	Add Container Insights integration for AKS into the IAC code.

CHAPTER 4

Performance Efficiency: Meet the Demand Spikes

Scaling up or down on demand to meet changing performance requirements is one of the major drivers of cloud adoption. This is in stark contrast to the on-premises approach where the planning has to be done up front to meet peak performance demands. As we discussed in Chapter 2, over-provisioning is an anti-pattern that should be avoided in the cloud to optimize the costs. How do you strike a balance between the performance demands and cost optimization? This chapter will explore the paradigms for designing environments to meet varying performance demands, while ensuring you stay within the budgeted cloud usage.

Design Principles for Performance Efficiency

The performance of your applications is measurable at a high level using three metrics: throughput of operations, latency experienced by users, and availability of the application. Depending on the nature of the application,

© Shijimol Ambi Karthikeyan 2021
S. Ambi Karthikeyan, *Demystifying the Azure Well-Architected Framework*,
https://doi.org/10.1007/978-1-4842-7119-3_4

there could be multiple service-level objectives (SLOs) that can help you measure performance efficiency.

- – Latency, or the time taken for the system to process requests

- – Throughput, or the number of requests that can be handled by the system in a unit of time

- – Margin of error, or the acceptable percentile of exceptions

Designing your environment for performance efficiency can be based on the following principles:

1. **Identify the right performance parameters from data.**

   Assumptions never work well in production deployments. Gather as much as data possible on your application performance requirements. Run diagnostics tools and analyze the data to reach conclusions. For example, if migrating from on-premises to the cloud, run performance assessment tools like the MAP tool or Azure Migrate that can monitor the performance of systems for a longer duration to identify the performance metrics. You can use this information to select the right services in the cloud, their SKUs, and scalability configurations.

2. **Stay away from performance anti-patterns.**

   While designing your applications, try to stay away from common anti-patterns that could bring down your application performance. The tried-and-tested patterns for one application may not work well for another application. Another common mistake is to follow the same patterns as on-premises for cloud-hosted applications. Microsoft has released a list of anti-patterns for performance that you should take into account for your application design, shown here:

- Busy database pattern resulting from database processing overload

- Too many background threads, affecting front-end response time for users

- Multiple small I/O requests over the network instead of lesser but larger requests

- Increased I/O overheads through extraneous data fetching, i.e., requests that fetch more data than required

- Creating multiple instances of objects and destroying them on demand, rather than instantiating them once and reusing them throughout the life of the application

- Resource contentions due to consolidation of all application data types to one data store

- Fetch the same data many times without implementing data caches leading to I/O overheads and throttling

- Multiple connection retries that could overwhelm the target service, rendering it unresponsive

- Impair scalability by blocking a thread waiting for the I/O operation to complete

3. **Plan for peak performance capacity through testing.**

Often applications that work fine in test environments fail in production when are hit by the peak workload. This is due to lack of proper load testing. There are a number of Microsoft-provided functionalities as well as third-party tools that you can leverage for load testing. Monitoring application under peak performance will help you avoid pitfalls like under-provisioning and over-provisioning. You can identify the baseline capacity for your applications as well as metrics that should trigger autoscaling to handle peak hour traffic.

4. **Maintain the cost performance balance.**

While designing for performance, ensure that there are no trade-offs with cost. For this you need to understand the billing meters associated with the Azure resources used in the architecture in order to calculate your monthly cloud bill. The SKU of the component will determine the base pricing, but there would be multiple meters associated with the resource that add to the cost. For example, the storage account would have additional meters like standard I/O and a data transfer rate in addition to the storage capacity, and the cost would vary based on the storage tier being used.

5. **Implementing continuous monitoring and optimization.**

Managing performance efficiency is an ongoing process that happens throughout the lifecycle of the application. As with other WAF pillars, continuous monitoring and optimization is a non-negotiable to achieve this. Identify the relevant application, infrastructure, data access, and other metrics relevant for your application and implement a process for continuous improvement based on the outcome. This is also important to readjust the base SKUs over time as well as the thresholds set of autoscaling. We will deep dive into monitoring metrics for performance later in this chapter.

Design Process

Figure 4-1 shows a high-level workflow of designing your application for performance efficiency.

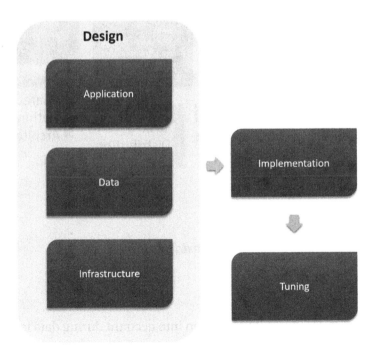

Figure 4-1. *Performance efficiency workflow*

Application

Let's start with the application design. The application should ensure scalability with factors such as workload partitioning, task distribution, and a shared-nothing approach factored into the design.

Figure 4-2 summarizes the key considerations while designing applications for peak performance.

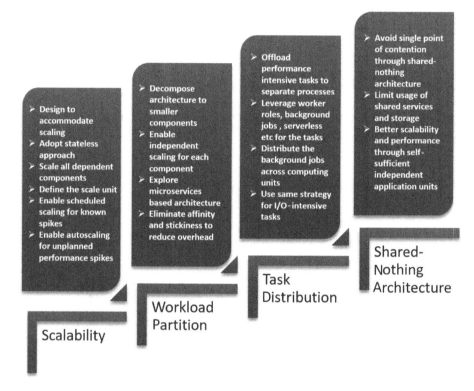

Figure 4-2. *Peak performance considerations*

Data

The most important factors to be taken into account during data layer design include partitioning, consistency, denormalization, caching, and optimization, as shown in Figure 4-3.

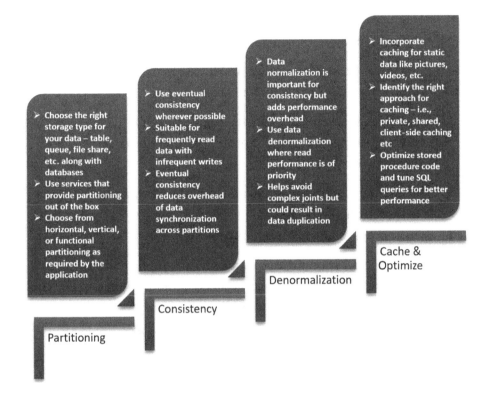

Figure 4-3. *Data layer design considerations*

The following additional aspects are also important to fine-tune data layer performance:

- Reduce heavy load targeting services by implementing queue-based load leveling between the task and the service.

- Offload data processing as much as possible to the application logic rather than doing it within the data store.

- Avoid queries that retrieve a massive amount of data, and optimize queries by selecting the right columns and rows.

- Reduce multiple calls to the database; combine related query operations or use stored procedures.

- Leverage Azure blob storage and the Azure content delivery network to cache static content.

- Reduce the size of data transfer objects (DTOs) between application layers to eliminate overhead on the network.

- Implement archival policies and move less frequently accessed data to cold or archival tiers of cloud storage to improve efficiency and reduce storage cost.

- Leverage data compression strategies to optimize the network traffic and improve application performance. Use tools such as Azure Frontdoor or built-in compression methods of application frameworks.

Infrastructure

Figure 4-4 summarizes how using the right infrastructure layer components plays a crucial role in the overall performance efficiency of the application. This includes using the right services for compute, storage, and networking and enabling the integration between different application components.

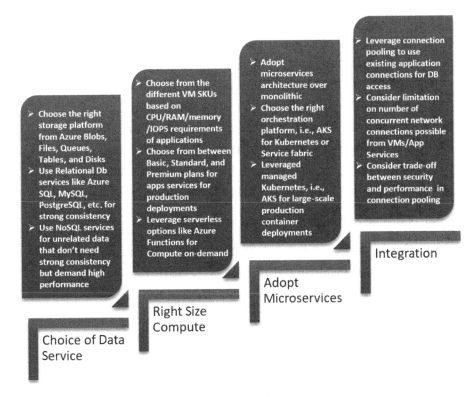

Figure 4-4. *Infrastructure layer considerations*

Make Best Use of Cloud Scalability

Scalability and performance are closely related. To increase performance on demand, your application design should be scalable. As you increase the units of compute, storage, or network, the performance should increase proportionally. In dynamic environments, autoscaling should be adapted to meet changing performance demands.

Let's explore some of the design considerations for scaling.

1. **Consider the future capacity requirements.**

   Start with baselining your current workloads, but you need to take into account the long-term strategy of your application and predicted usage of it. You might start with a base SKU, but over time you would have to scale up or scale out based on usage. Conduct performance testing to identify the capacity limits (we will be discussing this in the next section of this chapter). For multiregion architectures, consider the overall capacity required in all regions and any constraints on it, such as the availability of additional SKUs to increase capacity.

2. **Choose between scaling up and scaling out.**

Depending on the scale targets, choose between horizontal (scale out) and vertical (scale up) scaling. In vertical scaling, the size of the existing system is increased. This will often result in a downtime, so should be considered only when systems are designed for high availability. Horizontal scaling, on the other hand, adds additional instances to handle increased load. This requires the application to be designed in such a way that all instances can handle the load in a distributed manner. You should understand the time taken for the scaling to happen and the possibility of degraded performance for the application until the scaling is complete.

3. **Determine the unit of scale.**

Interdependent components are often scaled as a single unit. For example, when the front-end VM or app service is scaled, you need to add scale instances for all subsequent tiers including the databases. If there is an upper scaling limit for any resources, consider using deployment stamp patterns. For example, the group of resources in one geography catering to customers in that region can be mapped to a deployment stamp and can be scaled together.

4. **Identify the metrics for autoscaling.**

   Autoscaling is the process of scaling out resources automatically to meet varying performance demands. They are trigged by a predefined set of metrics. For Azure Virtual Machine Scale Sets (VMSS), Azure App Services, and Azure Cloud Services, it is enabled through the Azure Monitor autoscale feature. You can scale resources based on a schedule or runtime metrics like spikes in CPU/ memory usage. The same metrics can be monitored to scale down resources once the peak usage is over.

Figure 4-5 shows a sample autoscaling configuration for VMSS, which scales out or scales in VMs based on the CPU utilization percentage, which is one of the Azure Monitor autoscale metrics.

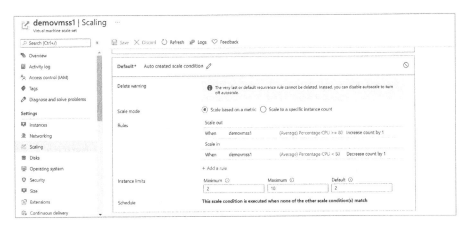

Figure 4-5. *Autoscaling for VMSS*

Figure 4-6 shows a sample autoscaling configuration for Azure App Services. Note that the scaling is scheduled for specific days in the week, i.e., preemptive scaling. For example, consider an ecommerce website that could experience heavy traffic on weekends.

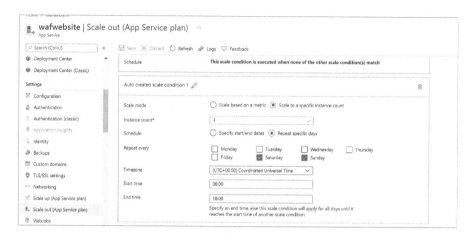

Figure 4-6. *Autoscaling for Azure App Services*

Identify Bottlenecks Through Performance Testing

Performance testing focuses on the nonfunctional aspects of applications to ensure that it can still be responsive when there is a considerable increase in user requests or other back-end activities. There are many tools like JMeter, OpenSTA, LoadRunner, WebLOAD, etc., that can be used for the performance testing of your application. Performance testing is not done to identify defects in the application, but rather to ensure a satisfactory user experience. It has to be done before your application hits production and is not a one-time activity. Before releasing any new updates, performance tests will help to ensure that the quality of the application experience is not disrupted by the change.

Figure 4-7 summarizes the considerations while planning for performance testing.

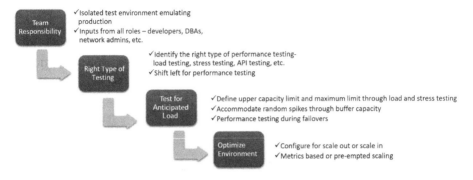

Figure 4-7. *Performance testing considerations*

− Ensure that the team is aligned on the test goals and you have a test environment ready.

− As defined by DevOps principles, there is no demarcation of roles. Along with the QA team, the developers, architects, and infrastructure team all have a role to play in making the tests successful.

− Ensure that there is test coverage for all aspects of the application, i.e., code, infrastructure automation, resiliency, etc.

− Start early with the testing cycle and not before the production deployment. This "shift-left" approach with performance testing will help identify issues earlier in the application lifecycle.

− Integrate testing tools with DevOps processes. Consider tools like JMeter, K6, and Selenium for this.

We touched upon testing in brief in Chapter 3 while discussing application design for operational excellence. Let's now look into features of tests that are non-negotiable from a performance efficiency point of view.

Load testing: This is the most important test that benchmarks system behavior when the application usage increases. Figure 4-8 shows the main considerations.

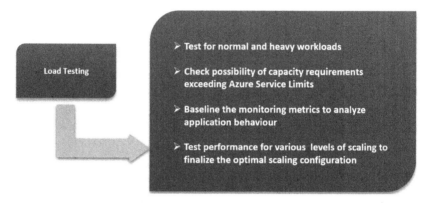

Figure 4-8. *Load testing considerations*

Stress testing: Stress testing is done to determine the upper limit of tolerance for applications. Figure 4-9 shows the main consideration.

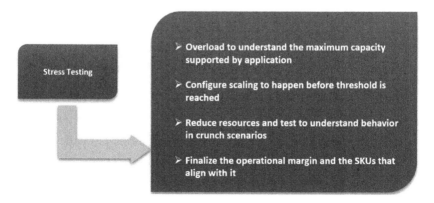

Figure 4-9. *Stress testing considerations*

Multiregion testing: Multiregion architectures would also need extensive performance testing to ensure that customers accessing application components hosted in primary or secondary regions do not experience any impediments. Figure 4-10 shows the main considerations for the testing.

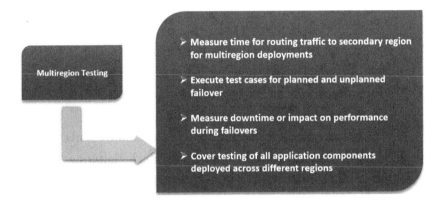

Figure 4-10. Multiregion testing cosiderations

Monitoring Metrics for Performance

Monitoring for performance should cover the aspects of scalability, reliability, application, and infrastructure monitoring along with correlation and interpretation of monitoring data.

- Leverage multidimensional metrics from Azure Monitor for additional context of monitoring data. You can stream data from different sources to log analytics to derive further insights. This could include data from external SIEM tools or from Application Insights as well.

- Monitor the data from different sources such as application logs, OS performance metrics, Azure resource metrics, events from service health, or Azure AD logs for a 360-degree view of your deployments. Performance issues can be traced back to multiple sources, and hence a holistic view of application health is important.

- Application Insights is custom-built to provide comprehensive application performance monitoring. Your application can be instrumented to enable a focused detection of components that are creating performance bottlenecks. It also helps correlate events from different layers of the application stack, helping you to pinpoint issues at a transaction level.

- Along with application monitoring using Application Insights, all infrastructure components should have diagnostics enabled with data forwarded to aggregation tools such as log analytics. This is applicable for all IaaS and PaaS services as well as third-party NVAs included in the architecture.

- Define the "healthy" and "unhealthy" status of application components and include enough leeway in the monitoring process to detect transient failures.

- Leverage an "application map" service to pinpoint performance issues in a distributed application. The "investigate performance" option from the application map helps you to drill down deeper into performance issues associated with application components.

Use Case Analysis

Let's revisit the ecommerce case study that was introduced in Chapter 1 for the retail industry. The optimal customer experience is one of the key requirements here, and it is important to ensure that the application is designed for peak performance.

Scenario 2

Industry: Retail

Ecommerce has become a key enabler for the retail industry. It is a highly competitive arena, so customers are spoiled by all the choices. Ecommerce websites should be designed for optimal customer experience to ensure repeatable business. The Azure Well-Architected Framework can help by identifying the right components for hosting, scaling, and securing ecommerce solutions and also to ensure long-term sustainability. Here are some key considerations for the scenario:

- Regular updates of catalogs to cover new product releases

- Secure payment transactions and storage personal information

- Quick retrieval of specific product information and possible alternatives

- Search experience personalized to customer preferences and previous purchases

- Capability to handle peak hour traffic such as Black Friday sales

Figure 4-11 shows a basic ecommerce web app architecture available in Azure Architecture Center. Note that this has to be customized further as per the business requirements of the customer. For example, intelligent product search can be enabled by integrating Azure Cognitive Services.

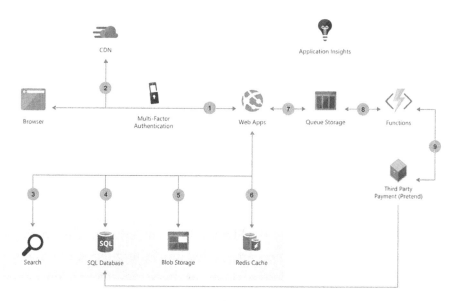

Figure 4-11. *Sample Architecture (Image courtesy: Azure Architecture Center)*

Table 4-1 summarizes some of the key considerations for performance efficiency while finalizing the architecture pattern for this use case.

Table 4-1. *Performance efficiency considerations*

Consideration	Rationale
Where geography does the customer plan to deploy the solution?	Ensure the proximity of the solution to the customer base to reduce access latency.
Is multiregion deployment required?	Identify if you need an active-active or active-passive deployment and whether you are going to route traffic to the target customer base in each geography.

(continued)

Table 4-1. (*continued*)

Consideration	Rationale
Do you have well-defined performance goals?	Identify the level of performance you want to deliver to the customer and how it can be delivered through the different application components.
What are the scaling requirements of the application?	The ecommerce application is expected to have a spike in usage during holiday and sales seasons. Identify the metrics that can be used to trigger the autoscaling of the web app.
Is a CDN being considered to enhance the user experience?	Load static images in the CDN so that they can be loaded faster.
How do you plan the scalability of the data layer?	Finalize the consistency required for the data, and use database sharding as appropriate.
How do you ensure the right sizing of the compute component?	Select the base SKU of compute components like Azure Web Apps and Azure Functions. Enable autoscaling for Web Apps.
Have your factored in performance tuning for SQL?	Optimize the database queries and indexes for performance efficiency.
Have you defined the scale units for the application?	Define the scale units to take into account the different components that need to be scaled together to avoid performance-specific bottlenecks.
How is serverless being integrated into the architecture?	Azure Functions is used for on-demand activities like order payment.
Have you factored in the network connectivity limitations?	Consider the maximum concurrent connection limits supported by the App Services SKU and whether it can handle the current and future user base.

(*continued*)

Table 4-1. (*continued*)

Consideration	Rationale
Is load testing and stress testing conducted before production deployment?	Check whether the component SKUs and scalability configuration can handle heavy workloads or if it would exceed the Azure Service limits.
What are the metrics monitored by Application Insights?	Consider relevant metrics such as the server response times, browser exceptions, etc., along with application log monitoring and correlation.
Are you leveraging an application map to connect deeper insights to component performance issues?	Monitor the round-trip time from the front-end web app to other dependent components like SQL and Azure storage to pinpoint performance bottlenecks.
What is the acceptable performance degradation during disaster recovery scenarios?	Measure the time and impact on performance while routing traffic to a secondary region for multiregional deployments.

Key Takeaways

Performance efficiency has a direct impact on user experience, and managing it can make or break your cloud deployments. The scalability and capacity management of applications plays a key role in ensuring the desired level of performance. Identify the right metrics and incorporate autoscaling as much as possible. Test all aspects of the application covering the code, data, and infrastructure early from the application lifecycle to avoid last-minute surprises. Use native monitoring solutions to flag and correlate events that could indicate performance bottlenecks.

CHAPTER 5

Reliability: Build Resilient Applications in the Cloud

The practical approach for ensuring resiliency in the cloud is to assume that failures will happen and plan for them from the design phase. Many of the Azure services have redundancy features available out of the box, but they need to be enabled as per application requirements. Having redundant configurations does not make the cut if they compromise the other pillars such as cost optimization and operational excellence. Adopting the right strategy to resiliency that can meet your defined service level agreements (SLAs) should be your prime focus. This chapter will focus on considerations for building resilient and highly available applications in Azure.

Design Principles for Resiliency

Adding resource instances before the "go live" of an application as an afterthought is not the right approach for ensuring resiliency. You need to ensure that resiliency is factored in from day 1, and the design principles listed here can be used as reference points:

© Shijimol Ambi Karthikeyan 2021
S. Ambi Karthikeyan, *Demystifying the Azure Well-Architected Framework*,
https://doi.org/10.1007/978-1-4842-7119-3_5

1. **Quantify the availability targets.**

   Availability targets cannot be abstract definitions.
   You should quantify them using SLAs and service
   level objectives (SLOs) so that they can be
   measurable. Despite all best efforts, failures can
   happen, so you should also define the acceptable
   downtime and the data loss, i.e., recovery point
   objective (RPO) and recovery time objective (RTO),
   for the application. Note that there are probably
   financial penalties associated with not meeting
   the SLAs/SLOs or recovery times. Hence, the
   application resiliency strategy should be defined
   and thoroughly tested against these targets.

2. **Ensure application, data, and infrastructure
   reliability.**

   Resiliency is not just limited to the infrastructure
   or application connectivity. It should be covered
   from the ground up, from the infrastructure up to
   the application and data layer. All these factors can
   impact the user experience and overall resiliency
   of the application. For example, having failover
   connectivity and multiple instances hosting
   the application will not ensure resiliency if the
   underlying database has a single point of failure.

3. **Ensure reliability in performance.**

   We discussed in much detail performance and
   scalability in the previous chapter. Applications
   while being resilient should also be able to scale
   on demand to meet increased application access
   demand, all the while maintaining acceptable levels

of performance. There could be brief unavailability of services during the scaling process, which should be factored into the reliability design.

4. **Manage the security risks that could impact resiliency.**

   Security vulnerabilities could take down your applications if not addressed proactively. If an attacker is able to infiltrate the application, it could lead to downtime irrespective of the number of additional resources you might have deployed for resiliency. Organizations should follow the security best practices for respective Azure services in addition to configuring them for resiliency.

5. **Set up automated lifecycle management.**

   For large-scale enterprise deployments, managing the resiliency of resources manually is not a scalable option. Ensure that the principles of operational excellence (discussed in Chapter 3) are followed while managing the lifecycle of application components. Resiliency-related configurations should be automated and also evaluated in the testing plan for the application.

6. **Design to recover from failure.**

   Ensure that an automated recovery mechanism is factored into the application design so that it can recover gracefully from failures. It should be aligned with the defined SLA/SLO or RPO/RTO targets. The application should be able to recover from component failures as well as catastrophic disasters affecting, say, an entire cloud region. Different applications will have different appetites for downtime based on their defined availability target. Consider all these factors while designing an application for resiliency.

7. **Implement continuous monitoring and optimization.**

As with all the other pillars of the Well-Architected Framework, monitoring your environments against the defined resiliency targets and continuously optimizing your configurations to meet the desired target are vital tasks. Lack of proper monitoring and trend analysis could lead to unexpected availability issues directly impacting resiliency targets.

Popular Adoption Strategies to Meet the Defined SLAs

Start with your availability and recovery target as the North Star for resilient system design. There are two main aspects to be considered here.

- Building resilient applications that can recover from failure

- High availability of all application components to serve user requests

Be aware of the cost implications associated with high availability. Start with a proper assessment of the high availability business case. The target SLAs and SLOs may not be applicable to all instances of the applications, say, for example, the test and dev environments. However, it would be non-negotiable for production deployments.

Considerations While Defining Application SLAs

Service level agreements define the acceptable levels of performance and availability for an application. When it comes to complex and distributed applications, there will be several moving parts that contribute to the overall resiliency of the application.

- Map the dependency of the application SLA with the SLA of all associated components and calculate the composite SLA. The SLA of all critical application components and related dependencies should be factored in to set realistic availability targets.

- Enable monitoring to measure the mean time between failures (MTBF). This helps to serve as a reality check on the SLAs you have defined and readjust them practically.

- Define the availability targets during DR failovers. If they are the same as during normal operations, you will have to invest in additional components for resiliency in the DR region as well.

- Define the "failed" state when the action plan for resiliency has to be triggered. It could be the degraded performance of components that would need additional instances to be created to replace the existing ones or even trigger a failover to a different region.

Conduct Failure Mode Analysis

Failure mode analysis (FMA) helps to identify the weak links or the failure points in your application. Adopt a shift-left strategy where FMA is done early in the lifecycle to identify the weak links, the possibility of failure, and the strategy for their recovery. Before we look into the FMA process, let's understand the key terminology associated with it.

- *Fault point*: This consists of the components of applications that could fail, impacting availability.

- *Fault mode*: This describes the different possibilities of failure for a fault point.

- *Single point of failure*: This describes the component that can take down the entire application if it fails.

Figure 5-1 shows the process for FMA at a high level.

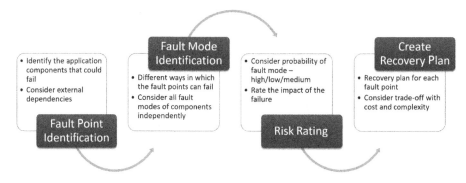

Figure 5-1. *FMA process*

Table 5-1 lists some examples of fault points, fault nodes, and their recovery plan. Note that you will have to create a similar plan for all identified fault points for your application.

Table 5-1. *Fault Points, Fault Node, and Recovery Plan*

Fault Point	Fault Mode	Recovery Plan
App Service	App unloaded while being idle	Enable "Always on" setting in web app to prevent unloading.
	Shut down by operator	Configure ReadOnly resource lock.
	App VM unavailable	App service is automatically restarted.
	Multiple bad requests from user	Leverage the API Management service to throttle user requests or block the user.
	App service breaks down due to an update	Roll back to the previous version through staging/production deployment slots.
Cosmos DB	Data read failures	1) Automated retry attempts. 2) Configure the maximum wait time. 3) Increase the throughput value of collection. 4) Set the preferredLocations parameter to send all reads to the first available Azure region.
	Data write failures	1) Automated retry attempts. 2) Increase throughput value of collection. 3) Multiregion replication. 4) Use a document backup queue for writes that can be processed later.

(*continued*)

Table 5-1. (*continued*)

Fault Point	Fault Mode	Recovery Plan
Azure SQl DB	DB connection fails	1) Enable active georeplication. 2) Update the connection string of the replica in the application.
	Number of connections to connection pool exhausted	1) Retry the connection. 2) Increase the available connection pools.
	Max connection limit reached	1) Retry the connection for transient failures. 2) Scale up the database SKU for persistent failures.

(*continued*)

Table 5-1. (*continued*)

Fault Point	Fault Mode	Recovery Plan
Service Bus	Read from Service bus fails	1) Connection retries. 2) Use dead-letter queue to store messages until they are retrieved.
	Write to Service bus fails	1) Automated retries. 2) Implement circuit breaker pattern to avoid retries in loop when quota is exceeded. 3) Improve resiliency by using partitioned queues/topics so that messages are distributed across multiple messaging stores. 4) Use multi region architecture with active or passive replication pattern.
	Duplicate messages	1) Use idempotent message processing pattern. 2) Set the `RequiredDuplicateDection` attribute to true while creating queues to detect duplicates.
	Unable to process message from queue	1) Configure a receiver to move the message to dead-letter queue. 2) Use `peeklock` mode so that a message is made available to other receivers if the message processing by one receiver fails.

(*continued*)

Table 5-1. (*continued*)

Fault Point	Fault Mode	Recovery Plan
Azure VM	VM connectivity error	1) Deploy a minimum of two VMs in an availability set/zone behind a load balancer. 2) Configure retry for transient errors. 3) Implement a circuit breaker pattern for nontransient error. 4) Scale out if the network egress limit is reached.
	Unhealthy/unavailable VMs	1) Deploy a minimum of two VMs in an availability set/zone behind a load balancer.
	Accidental shutdown of VMs	1) Enable read-only locks for VM. 2) Restrict the number of administrators and implement the principle of least privilege.
Azure Storage	Storage write errors	1) Configure retry for transient errors. 2) Perform graceful fallback to local cache or compensate the transaction in case of transactional scope.
	Storage read error	1) Configure retry for transient errors. 2) Use RA-GRS storage use the storage SDK to enable read from the secondary endpoint. 3) Implement graceful failback after retry limit exceeds.

Adoption Strategies

As reiterated earlier, the reliability of the application is the sum total of the reliability of its components. The adoption strategy for ensuring reliability will be dependent on the components, their availability in targeted Azure regions, their Azure service limits, etc. Some of the best practices that will help design resilient applications are listed in this section.

Place application components in a single region within an availability zone or in multiple regions for additional resiliency. Figure 5-2 shows regional resiliency considerations.

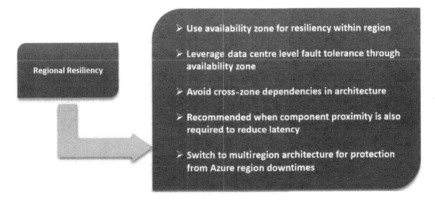

Figure 5-2. *Regional resiliency considerations*

An important step to ensure resiliency is to define how application components will respond to failures and their priority for recovery during an eventuality. For example, you need to decide which application components should be mandatorily protected, which components are nice to protect, and which components are ephemeral. Figure 5-3 shows the considerations for managing failures.

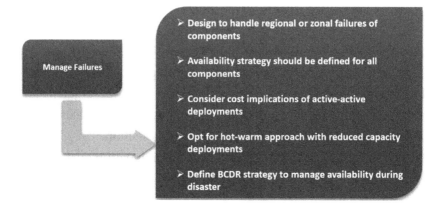

Figure 5-3. *Managing Failures*

Holistic dependency management is required to ensure the reliability of applications. It includes internal dependencies of components within the application and external dependencies on other Azure or third-party services. Figure 5-4 highlights key considerations for dependency management.

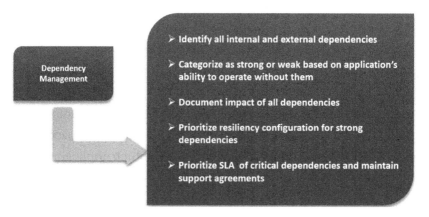

Figure 5-4. *Dependency management considerations*

Testing and Monitoring

All application updates or architecture changes should go through a stringent resiliency test process. There are different kinds of tests that can be conducted to test the resiliency of your application stack. Let's explore some of the crucial ones.

Test Strategies

The why, why, and how of testing is important to ensure the resiliency of your systems. Consider the following best practices while testing your application for reliability:

- Start with a well-defined testing plan covering all fault modes and fault points.

- Define a DR strategy. Focus on running applications with reduced functionality to manage unplanned outages.

- Automate the failover and failback steps as much as possible to reduce the turnaround time.

- Select the right types of tests that suit your application reliability requirements.

- Test regularly to measure the effectiveness against defined targets and thresholds.

- Create dedicated environments for testing, closely simulating production. Subsets of tests might also be run in production with a controlled blast radius.

Chaos engineering: This is the approach of injecting faults in systems and then monitoring the impact to gauge application resiliency. This could include shutting down services/VMs, forcing failovers, changing access restrictions, etc. Figure 5-5 shows the key considerations.

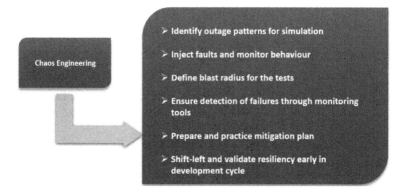

Figure 5-5. *Chaos Engineering considerations*

Peak load testing: The application has to stay resilient under peak workloads. However, the scenarios have to be simulated and tested regularly through peak load testing to monitor how the components would behave. Figure 5-6 summarizes the key considerations for effective peak load testing.

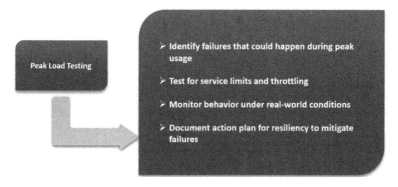

Figure 5-6. *Peak load testing considerations*

Backup and DR testing: While having a well-defined business continuity/disaster recovery plan is a priority, without regular testing it would not help you in real-world scenarios. Figure 5-7 summarizes key considerations for effective Backup & DR testing.

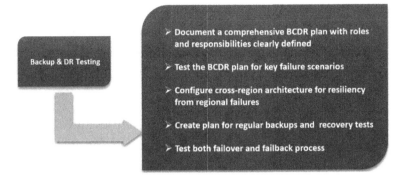

Figure 5-7. *Backup & DR testing considerations*

Monitoring and Optimization

Monitoring services will help provide real-time visibility into the status of your application's health and identify incidents that could impact the overall resiliency of the system. Consider the following guidelines to ensure resiliency while you configure monitoring for your applications:

– Consider the service limits of Azure subscriptions and monitor for any components that could cross the limit. Alerts triggered can be leveraged to horizontally or vertically scale the respective components before the service throttles and impacts the availability of the application.

– Instrument your application to detect possible failures that could have an adverse effect on application availability. Ensure that dependent services are monitored and behaviors are correlated to get a view of the overall application health.

–   Use tools like Application Insights and Log Analytics to
    collate data from different sources and derive insights
    from it. You can also leverage recommendations from
    Azure Monitor to improve your system reliability and
    performance.

–   Configure alerts based on monitoring metrics and
    send them to the operations team. You can also enable
    auto-remediation for the alerts by using runbooks or
    by calling webhooks that could trigger the remediation
    plan. Include service-level alerts that could notify you
    of any service degradation along with specific Azure
    resource alerts focused on resource-level events.

–   Configure the right threshold for alerts to avoid false
    alarms. Some of the issues could be transient, and
    hence it is appropriate to implement application
    retry logic to handle them. Persistent issues should
    be flagged by monitoring alerts so that additional
    remediation plans can be initiated.

–   Configure and customize dashboards to get a bird's-
    eye view of your application health. This could include
    individual resource metrics and graphs from tools such
    as Azure Application Insights, Log Analytics, Azure
    Monitor, etc. Figure 5-8 shows a sample dashboard for
    an application.

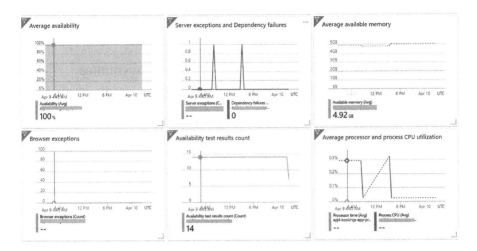

Figure 5-8. *Application health sample dashboard*

Use Case Analysis

Let's revisit the financial case study that was introduced in Chapter 1. Resiliency is the most crucial aspect of applications in this sector as huge financial transactions could be impacted due to the unviability of systems. It is important to ensure that the application is designed to overcome transient as well as persistent failures.

Scenario 4

Industry: Financial

Most financial-sector organizations such as banks and insurance companies are faced with challenges of adapting their legacy systems to cloud. There could be some hard dependencies, but most of them can be circumvented by leveraging the right pillars of the Well-Architected Framework. Here are some key considerations of using the Well-Architected Framework while migrating financial-sector line-of-business (LOB) applications to Azure:

- Identity integration for seamless experience, for both customers and employees

- Resiliency of workloads migrated to Azure; downtimes can be unacceptable for banking solutions

- Leveraging PaaS services for modernizing some of the legacy components

- Security of data at rest after migration and in transit during migration

- Flexibility to adopt hybrid architectures; some components might still remain on-premises due to security/compliance reasons

- Visibility into security posture of the environment post migration, identifying malicious activities, and doing proactive remediation

Figure 5-9 shows a multitenant software-as-a-service architecture designed for high availability that is available in Azure Architecture Center. Note that this has to be customized further as per the business requirements of the customer, such as using Key Vault to store and retrieve secrets.

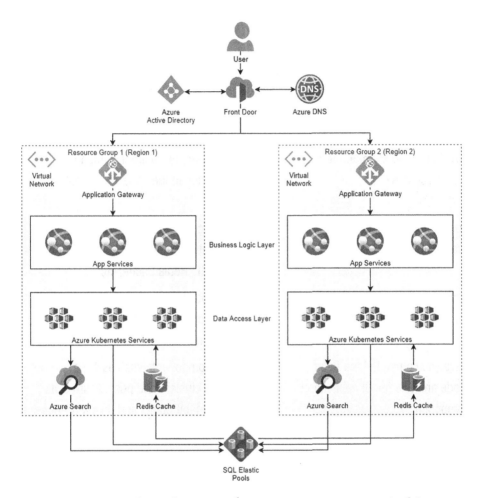

Figure 5-9. *Sample Architecture (Image courtesy: Azure Architecture Center)*

Table 5-2 summarizes some of the key considerations for resiliency while finalizing the architecture pattern for this use case.

Table 5-2. *Considerations for Application Reliability*

Consideration	Rationale
What are the right-fit services to ensure the resiliency of the application?	Select components such as App Service, AKS, and Azure SQL that have high availability built in.
How is availability managed across regions?	Azure Front Door can redirect traffic to a secondary region in the case of regional failures.
Do you have well-defined availability goals?	Calculate the composite SLA while considering all the application components, App Service, AKS, Azure SQL, Redis Cache, etc.
Have you considered the Azure service availability and limits?	Develop a capacity model considering the availability and usage patterns of services in targeted regions.
Have you completed the failure mode analysis for all application components?	Consider all components such as Apps Services, AKS clusters and pods, Azure SQL, Redis, etc., as fault points and do a fault-node analysis.
Is there any single point of failure in the architecture?	Ensure that resiliency is built into all components, eliminating a single point of failure.
Have you defined a DR plan for the application and its components?	Along with configuring a multiregion architecture, ensure that there is a DR strategy defined for all application components for regional or zonal failure and network connectivity for hybrid connections (if applicable).

(continued)

Table 5-2. (*continued*)

Consideration	Rationale
Have you configured availability metrics in monitoring?	Configure health probes to monitor availability targets and alert stakeholders of any possible downtime.
How is the data layer redundancy handled?	Enable data replication across regions, segregate read operations from updates, configure health probes, and ensure application consistency in the event of a data corruption.
How is the infrastructure redundancy handled?	Configure health probes in the application gateway, monitor network traffic for outages, and run simulations to ensure connectivity during outages.
Have you built in scalability into the application components?	The application should remain available during peak usage by either scaling out or scaling up.
Have you defined the test strategy and cadence?	Ensure that you follow the principle of shift-left testing for components. Along with chaos engineering, DR testing and peak load testing should also be conducted regularly.
How is availability factored into the application logic?	Incorporate methods to handle faults, configure timeouts between components, and enable application instrumentation.
How are the operational processes defined, aligning them with reliability?	Automated end-to-end deployments for new updates; time is taken for redeployments in the event of a disaster; and rollback plans, etc., should be factored in.

Key Takeaways

Reliability is one of the key pillars of the Well-Architected Framework as managing application availability has a direct impact on your SLAs/SLOs. It could also impair user experiences leading to long-standing consequences. Organizations should define availability targets for key components and adopt the right strategy to ensure end-to-end resiliency. Additionally, continuous monitoring and testing of the services is also important to gain confidence on the resiliency of the design and optimize it as required.

CHAPTER 6

Security: Protect Your Workloads in the Cloud

Security paradigms in the cloud are different from traditional on-premises deployments where the focus was mostly on securing the network perimeter. In the cloud, the threat vectors are much more advanced, and so your security strategy has to be too. Security breaches would negatively impact the customer trust as well as your revenue. Hence, security is a non-negotiable aspect of any application architecture. This chapter will cover the practical aspects of enabling security to ensure the confidentiality and integrity of workloads in Azure.

Understanding Threat Vectors in the Cloud

Security in the cloud is always a challenging subject, especially with the shared responsibility model that needs to be followed. While some aspects of security such as the platform, data center, hardware, etc., are managed by Microsoft, the security of the application, data, and infrastructure (in the case of IaaS) is still owned by the customer. The threat vectors in the cloud are evolving by the day, so customers are required to be

© Shijimol Ambi Karthikeyan 2021

S. Ambi Karthikeyan, *Demystifying the Azure Well-Architected Framework*,
https://doi.org/10.1007/978-1-4842-7119-3_6

always on the lookout to protect their workloads by implementing the right security controls. Cybercriminals are always on the lookout for opportunities to attack: known vulnerabilities left unpatched, malware injection, in-memory malicious code execution, configuration drifts, etc. The information on the latest types of attacks is summarized and released periodically by Microsoft in security intelligence reports that can be downloaded from `https://www.microsoft.com/en-us/security/business/security-intelligence-report`.

There are different ways in which a malicious attacker can gain access to your applications in Azure.

1) *Unprotected perimeter*: Unrestrictive rules in perimeter devices like Azure Firewall, Network Virtual Appliance (NVA), or Network Security Group (NSG) can act as an invitation to cyber attackers to enter your cloud network and move laterally from there to exploit other systems.

2) *Malware attacks*: As with on-premise systems, malware attacks are commonplace in the cloud, and they provide the greatest return on investment (ROI) for the attackers. Banking Trojans, brute-force attacks targeting credentials, credential theft, launching ransomware, etc., are some of the common attack tactics of malware.

3) *Identity breaches*: Identity is truly the new security perimeter, as the control plane breach is the most common attack strategy in cyberspace. Identity thefts are more dangerous as attackers can impersonate a genuine user to wreak havoc in your cloud infrastructure or, even worse, steal business information unnoticed.

4) *Data thefts*: Though data in Azure is often protected by default through encryption, if attackers can get access to the keys, the data can easily be compromised. Hence, it is important to protect your encryption keys and also implement additional layers of security through identity-based access controls as well as network restrictions.

5) *Known vulnerabilities*: Internet-facing applications are more on the radar of cyber threats as there is a possibility of attackers trying to exploit known vulnerabilities like cross-site scripting or SQL injection.

6) *Configuration drifts*: Azure provides a set of security best practices for all services. Though organizations follow best practices during the initial implementation phase, it is a common trend for configuration drifts to happen during the application lifecycle, which could leave the doors open for attacks.

Adaptable Security for New-World Threats

Before we get into the right controls to be implemented to secure workloads in the cloud, let's take a moment to look into the shared responsibility model for security in Azure, as shown in Figure 6-1.

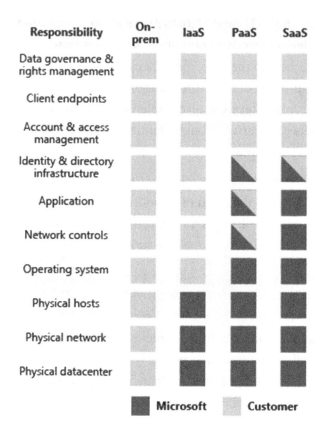

Figure 6-1. *Shared responsibility model for security (Image courtesy: Microsoft)*

The shared responsibility model provides a demarcation of controls to be implemented by the cloud service provider, i.e., Microsoft and the customer. Microsoft takes care of aspects such as physical infrastructure security, training for security staff, platform protection, staff background checks, access control, etc. The customer, on the other hand, is expected to take care of the OS/application/data layer security, access control, and data governance depending on whether the IaaS, PaaS, or SaaS model is being used.

Design Principles

Microsoft recommends a defense-in-depth security strategy to ensure the end-to-end security of your workloads. The rule of thumb is to assume a breach and build up a layer of defense against all possible attacks. Even if one of the layers is breached by the attacker, the infiltration should be prevented by subsequent layers. The principles that should guide your efforts on security are confidentiality, integrity, and availability. This is commonly known as the CIA triad.

- *Confidentiality*: Ensure that only authorized personnel have access to your data and applications by enabling the principle of least privilege.

- *Integrity*: The data being transferred between systems should be tamper-proof so that there is no compromise on the integrity either at rest or in transit. Any modifications should be tracked through hashing algorithms that can be used to ensure that the data was not tampered with.

- *Availability*: Along with application component failures, organized attacks like a distributed denial of service (DDoS) can impair the availability of your application for authorized users. Hence, preventing such eventualities is also a focus for security in Azure.

Figure 6-2 shows the different security layers that will protect your application and data.

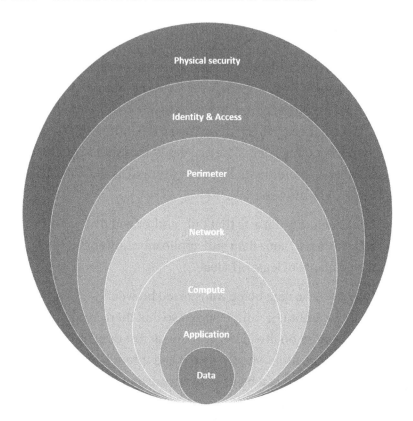

Figure 6-2. *Application and data security layers*

Table 6-1 summarizes how each of these layers can help in enabling the CIA triad.

Table 6-1. *CIA triad enablement*

Ring	Description	Principle
Data	Protect data stored in databases, in storage, or in SaaS applications through proper access control and encryption mechanisms.	Integrity
Application	Integrate security right from the design of the application, make sure the associated storage is secure, and scan the code for vulnerabilities.	Integrity
Compute	Protect virtual machines from vulnerabilities; ensure network security, endpoint protection, etc.	Availability, integrity
Network	Enable network segmentation; restrict traffic flow to only what is required.	Confidentiality, availability
Perimeter	Enable distributed denial-of-service protection, implement perimeter firewalls, and use NVAs to prevent network breaches.	Availability
Identity and access	Protect the control plane through role-based access control (RBAC) and protect identities through options like multifactor authentication.	Integrity
Physical security	This is the first line of defense, which is implemented by Microsoft to ensure that physical data centers are protected through proper access control, monitoring, and screening.	Confidentiality

To enable the security pillar of the Well-Architected Framework of your application, the following guidelines can be used:

1. **Develop a well-defined security strategy.**

   People, process, and technology should come together to enable comprehensive security for your workloads in Azure. This starts with coming up with a security strategy that encompasses all three. Invest in processes that ingrain security into an application by default and develop a security-first culture in your organization. The next step is to identify the security configurations and tools in Azure that will help you implement this strategy.

2. **Design from an attacker's perspective.**

Your security strategy has to be one step ahead and robust enough to protect you from what the attackers might be planning. Hence, you need to think like an attacker's to simulate attacks and measure the effectiveness of your security controls. Conduct penetration tests and attack simulations through red team exercises to understand the current attack surface and then reduce it.

3. **Leverage native security tools and configurations.**

The recommended approach for enabling security is to use the out-of-the-box services and features offered by the Azure platform. Customers who have a hybrid architecture might prefer to use the NVA corresponding to their on-premises security devices, especially if the third-party service offers a bring-your-own-license (BYOL) option. Using such tools ensures that you are considering the long-term roadmap of the product and integration requirements.

4. **Integrate resiliency into your security strategy.**

   Even with security controls applied, assume failure, and ensure that you have implemented a layered security strategy. There should be a primary security control and secondary security control as a backup should the primary fail. This is aligned with the defense-in-depth approach to security.

5. **Assume zero trust.**

   There should not be any unconditional access for any resources. Restrict access time through options like just-in-time access or shared access signature tokens and enhance trust validation through multifactor authentication. Any issues detected, such as leaked credentials, malware infections, etc., should be remediated in a timely manner to enforce security.

6. **Monitor and optimize.**

   As with all the other WAF pillars, monitoring and optimization are essential for the security pillar for continuous improvement. As threats in the cloud evolve, you need to integrate your learnings from the recent attacks, penetration testing, and red team simulation outcomes and strengthen the security strategy. You should also leverage Azure native tools such as Security Center, Azure Monitor, Azure Sentinel, Azure Defender, etc., for monitoring and detecting vulnerabilities.

Secure Infrastructure, Data, Network, and Application

Infrastructure forms the baseline of all your cloud deployments. Aligning the right processes, tools, and security strategy is important to strengthening this base.

1. **Infrastructure segmentation**

    The environments should be segmented and aligned with the business needs. Segmentation is not limited to network isolation; it also means creating a logical segregation through management groups, subscriptions, and resource groups. Role-based access control and policy assignments could be different across these segments. Figure 6-3 shows the main considerations while planning to segment your environment.

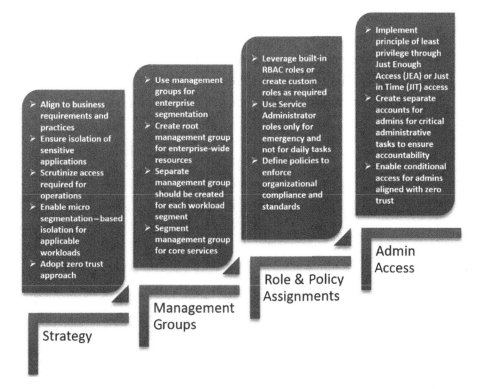

Figure 6-3. *Considerations for Infrastructure segmentation*

2. **Network security**

Ensure that network segmentation is created
based on the application architecture and how
the components need to communicate with each
other. Network segmentation should be defined to
secure the communications between perimeters so
that the blast radius is controlled in the event of an
infiltration. Native Azure features like Azure Virtual
Network (VNet), NSG, Application Security Group
(ASG), Azure Firewall, etc., can be used to enable
segmentation. When application components are
deployed in subnets within a network, ensure that

there are restrictions implemented in terms of the kind of traffic that traverses between them through NSGs, and ensure the traffic is monitored using flow logs. Figure 6-4 shows the main considerations while planning for network security for workloads.

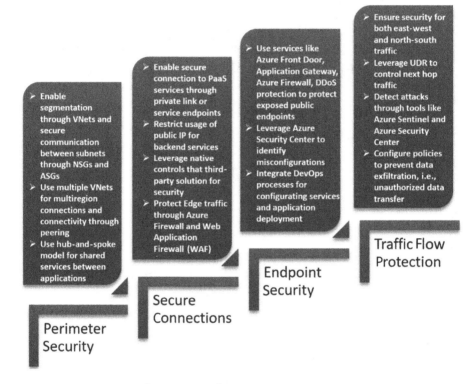

Figure 6-4. *Network security planning*

3. **Data protection**

Data can be protected at rest and in transit using the native security features in Azure. In addition to enabling encryption, identity-based storage access controls can be used to ensure the protection of data. Figure 6-5 lists the main considerations to enable data protection for workloads.

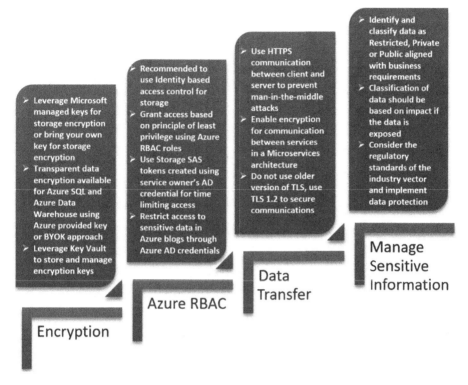

Figure 6-5. *Data protection considerations*

4. **Application security**

   Enabling security in applications involves
   protecting the hosting platform (in case of IaaS), the
   middleware, the code, and other components. Start
   with identifying high-risk, high-impact applications
   and strengthen the security posture of them. The
   dimensions of application security include identity,
   data protection, key management, application
   configuration management, and adherence to
   compliance standards. Figure 6-6 shows the main
   considerations to enable application security for
   workloads.

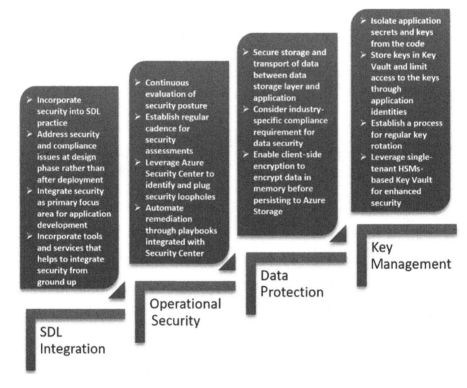

Figure 6-6. *Enabling application security for workloads*

Identity Is the New Security Perimeter

Identity has emerged as the security parameter in the cloud-first, mobile-first world where users could practically access applications from anywhere in the world from any device. This has led to the development of identity protocols supporting the diverse access patterns. However, if not secured properly, identity could become the weak link in your application ecosystem, enabling the attacker to sneak in undetected. Figure 6-7 summarizes the different aspects of protecting your identity in cloud.

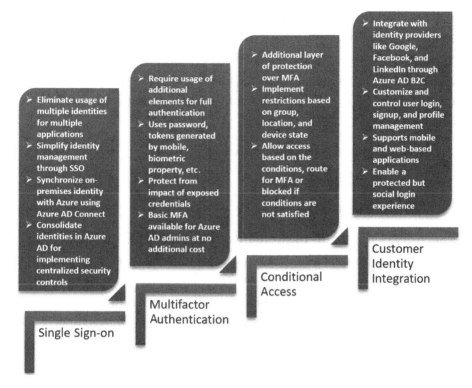

Figure 6-7. *Identity protection*

Azure Native Security Tools for Your SOC Team

Let's explore some of the native tools in Azure that can be leveraged by Security Operations Center (SOC) teams to detect and protect your workloads from security threats and anomalies.

Security Center: Azure Security Center provides cloud security posture management with a unified view into the state of security of your Azure resources. It focuses on protecting your workloads from quickly evolving security threats by ensuring that recommended best practices are adhered to and there are no misconfigurations. As cloud environments evolve quickly, it is also important to ensure that best practices are being followed when anyone deploys a new environment. Security Center focuses on the following to enable comprehensive security:

- Strengthening security posture

- Protecting against threats

- Getting secure faster

Security Center helps to strengthen the security posture by closing security loopholes, hardening services, and enforcing security policies. There are many built-in security policies that will help implement the security posture. Any new subscriptions created under the management group will automatically be covered under assigned polices that help address the security concerns associated with shadow IT subscriptions.

Figure 6-8 shows a sample Azure Security Benchmark policy assigned to a subscription, which looks into best practices such as the latest OS, Log Analytics agents' installation status, Log Analytics health issue resolution status, etc.

Home > Security Center > Security policy >

Azure Security Benchmark ⋯
Edit Initiative Assignment

Basics   **Parameters**   Remediation   Non-compliance messages   Review + save

Specify parameters for this initiative assignment.

Service principals should be used to protect your subscriptions instead of management certificates * ⓘ
AuditIfNotExists   ⌄

Operating system version should be the most current version for your cloud service roles * ⓘ
AuditIfNotExists   ⌄

Log Analytics agent health issues should be resolved on your machines * ⓘ
AuditIfNotExists   ⌄

Log Analytics agent should be installed on your virtual machine for Azure Security Center monitoring * ⓘ
AuditIfNotExists   ⌄

Log Analytics agent should be installed on your virtual machine scale sets for Azure Security Center monitoring * ⓘ
AuditIfNotExists   ⌄

Manage certificate validity period * ⓘ
disabled   ⌄

Figure 6-8. *Sample Azure Security Benchmark*

Azure Security Center continuously assesses your environment against
security best practices and compliance standards to provide a secure score
that quantifies your security posture, as shown in Figure 6-9.

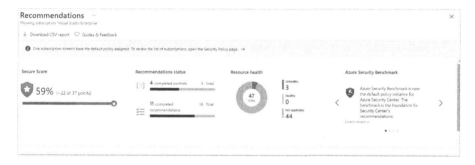

Figure 6-9. *Secure score*

The exact controls and action to be taken are also displayed in the
recommendations, as shown in Figure 6-10.

Controls		Max score	Current Score	Potential score increase	Unhealthy resources	Resource health	Actions
>	Enable MFA ⊘	10	10	+ 0% (0 points)	None		
>	Apply system updates ⊘	6	6	+ 0% (0 points)	None		
>	Manage access and permissions	4	0	+ 11% (4 points)	1 of 1 resources		
>	Enable encryption at rest	4	0	+ 11% (4 points)	2 of 2 resources		
>	Restrict unauthorized network access	4	0	+ 11% (4 points)	1 of 2 resources		
>	Remediate security configurations	4	2	+ 5% (2 points)	1 of 2 resources		
>	Apply adaptive application control ⊘	3	3	+ 0% (0 points)	None		
∨	Enable endpoint protection	2	1	+ 3% (1 point)	1 of 2 resources		
	Log Analytics agent should be installed on you... ⊘				None		
	Log Analytics agent health issues should be re... ⊘				None		
	Install endpoint protection solution on virtual ...				1 of 2 virtual machines		
>	Implement security best practices ⊘	Not scored	Not scored	+ 0% (0 points)	None		

Figure 6-10. *Recommendations*

Some of these recommendations can be directly implemented from Security Center. For example, endpoint threat protection can directly be enabled from the recommendations screen, as shown in Figure 6-11.

Home > Security Center > Recommendations >

Endpoint Protection not installed on Azure VMs ...   ✕

▽ Filter   ⬇ Install on 1 VMs

Virtual machine	↑↓ State ↑↓ Severity ↑↓
☑ laptopbackup	Open ❗ High •••

Figure 6-11. *Enabling recommendations*

In addition to enforcing and monitoring security policies, Azure Security Center can detect security threats in your environment and provide fusion kill-chain analysis to identity the details of the attack campaign, as shown in Figure 6-12.

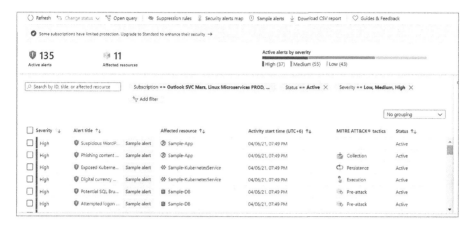

Figure 6-12. *Attack campaign insights*

If you click a specific alert, you can get more details of the vulnerability. Figure 6-13 shows sample alerts for an exposed Kubernetes Dashboard.

Figure 6-13. *Sample alert for Kubernetes Dashboard*

Security Center also provides prescriptive guidance on how to mitigate the vulnerability or even link to a logic app that can trigger an automated response, as shown in Figure 6-14.

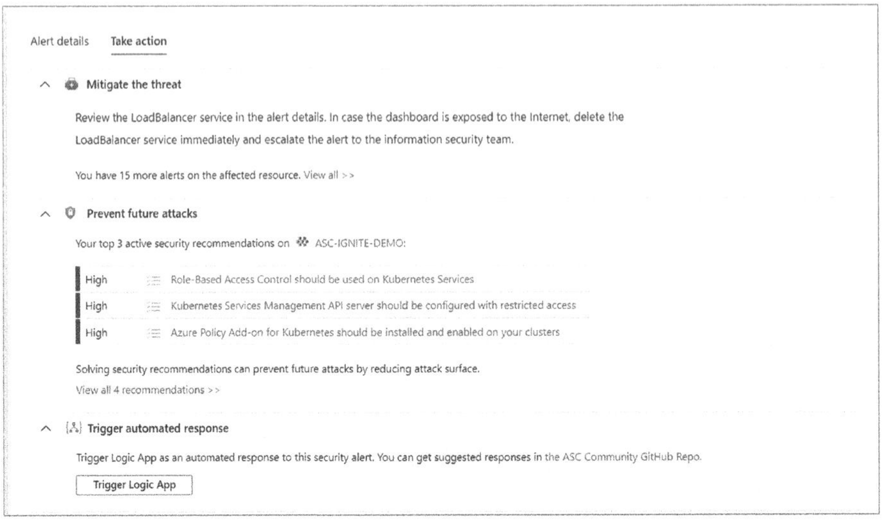

Figure 6-14. *Automated response*

Azure Security Center provides an organic way of managing the security of your workloads in Azure as all resources are automatically onboarded into the solution. This along with integrated Azure policies will help with the comprehensive security management of the workloads.

Azure Sentinel: This is the native security information event management (SIEM) and security orchestration automated response (SOAR) solution in Azure. The service can ingest logs from various sources including on-premises machines for security threat analytics and intelligence. It is a single-stop solution for in-depth visibility to threats, proactive hunting based on the MITRE framework, and threat visibility.

Figure 6-15 shows a sample incident overview from Azure Sentinel.

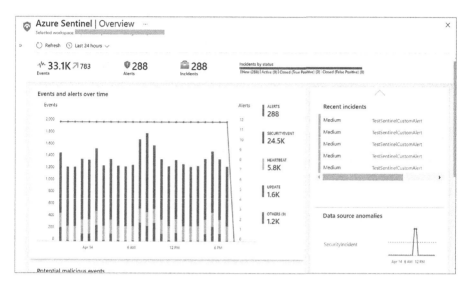

Figure 6-15. *Incident overview*

You can click a respective security event to get more details, as shown in Figure 6-16.

Figure 6-16. *Security event drilldown*

The Hunting queries in Azure Sentinel help to deliver insights for attacks proactively. You can run the Hunting queries available in Azure Sentinel, as shown in Figure 6-17, and further correlate them with other events.

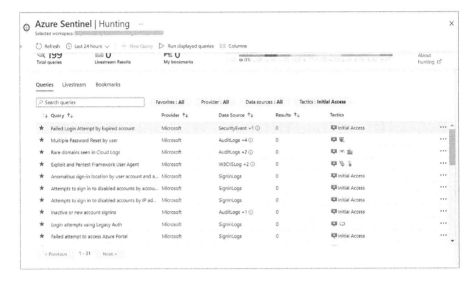

Figure 6-17. *Hunting queries*

Azure Defender: Azure Defender can be used for advanced threat detection for Windows and Linux machines. Threats detected by Azure Defender are consolidated and displayed in Azure Security Center for analysis and remediation. The services are automatically enabled in Windows servers onboarded to Security Center. The features provided by Azure Defender include just-in-time (JIT) VM access, file integrity monitoring, adaptive security controls, adaptive network hardening, Docker host hardening, fileless attack detection, Linux auditd alerts, and log analytics agent integration.

Use Case Analysis

Let's revisit the health and life sciences case study that was introduced in Chapter 1. Security is the most crucial aspect of applications in this sector, as it contains sensible customer information and any breaches to it can have a long-standing impact.

Scenario 1

Industry: Health and Life Sciences

With healthcare going digital, there are different options available for consumers such as fitness bands, online consultations, medication tracking, etc. A health and life sciences company can leverage the Well-Architected Framework while developing a cloud-based digital experience for its customers. Here are some key considerations for the scenario:

- There is lot of personally identifiable information (PII) involved, and hence data privacy and security are two of the primary concerns.

- The services should be accessible to customers when they need it and where they need it.

- The response time of applications should ensure a smooth customer experience.

- Adhere to HIPAA controls.

Figure 6-18 shows the sample architecture of a HIPAA- and HITRUST-compliant health AI solution.

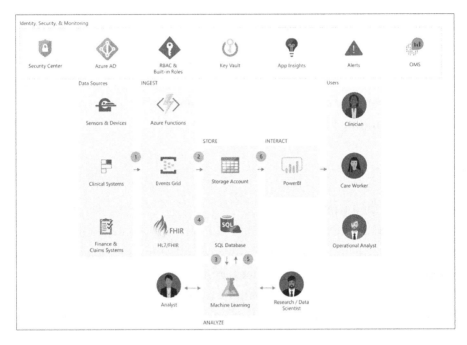

Figure 6-18. *Azure Architecture Center (Image courtesy: Azure Architecture Center)*

Table 6-2 lists some of the key considerations for security while finalizing the architecture pattern for this use case.

Table 6-2. *Considerations for Application Security*

Consideration	Rationale
Does the organization have a clear view on the access segregation for the application?	Identify the users and groups that need access to the application environment and their access level.
Is Azure RBAC configured as per the access requirements?	Manage the control plane access through RBAC for the users and groups identified.

(continued)

Table 6-2. (*continued*)

Consideration	Rationale
How is the authentication of the application configured?	Consider managed identities, implement password-less protection, and enable centralized identity management.
How is data at rest protected?	Leverage native data encryption for services and use Key Vault for key management.
How is data in transit protected?	Use TLS/HTTPs for communication between the application components and data layer.
How is storage access authenticated?	Enable fine-grained identity-based access control for storage.
Are the different possible threat vectors identified for the application?	Leverage threat modeling to risks associated with the application.
Are security measures integrated into the SDL cycle?	Use a shift-left approach to integrate security in your application code and evaluate the framework and application libraries for vulnerabilities.
Does the organization have a process defined to address alerts flagged by Security Center?	Use out-of-the-box features of Security Center and create processes for threat detection and remediation.
What are the compliance considerations for the workload?	Leverage Security Center to ensure that regulatory compliance controls are adhered to.
Does the organization have process defined to handle security incidents?	Configure alerts for security events and enable auto-remediation wherever possible.
What are the proactive measures taken to enable security?	Red team exercises and penetration testing need to be done periodically to identify weak links in the application architecture.

Key Takeaways

Security is the most crucial pillar of the Well-Architected Framework as vulnerabilities could easily pave the way to availability and data integrity issues. While Azure security is a vast topic and has many more dimensions than what can be covered in this chapter, we have discussed the non-negotiable considerations such as infrastructure, data, network, and application protection. Irrespective of how strongly you have implemented all the other WAF pillars for an application, security can easily make or break an application's impact and outcome. Hence, the organization should spend time focusing on developing a multidimensional security strategy for workloads in Azure.

Index

A

Application Security
   Group (ASG), 115
Azure Advisor, 34, 37
Azure Architecture Center, 79
Azure cloud cost
   management, 33, 34
Azure Cognitive Services, 79
Azure Kubernetes Service (AKS), 11
Azure Migrate, 33
Azure Monitor, 54, 55
Azure policies, 36
Azure Pricing Calculator
   app service, 30, 31
   cost differences, 30
   possible charges, 32
   updating details, 31
Azure Resource Consumption, 21
Azure Security Center, 57
Azure services, 17
Azure well-architected framework
   considerations, 5, 6
   cost optimization, 7
   operational excellence, 7
   performance efficiency, 8
   pillars, 9
   reliability, 8
   security, 9

B

Backup and DR testing, 96, 97
Blue-green deployment
   approach, 44
Bring-your-own-license (BYOL), 112
Build-Measure-Learn approach, 7

C

Canary release model, 44
Change failure rate (CFR), 41
Chaos engineering, 95, 96
Cloud Adoption Framework
   (CAF), 3, 5, 7
Cloud-based digital experience, 10
Cloud computing, 15
Cloud-native services, 5
Cloud Solution Provider (CSP), 3
Confidentiality, integrity, and
   availability (CIA), 109
Cost optimization
   architecture considerations,
      22–25
   Azure Migrate, 33
   Azure policies, 36
   Azure Pricing Calculator
      app service, 30, 31
      cost differences, 30

Cost optimization (*cont.*)
    possible charges, 32
    updating details, 31
  custom reports, 37
  design principles, 20
    budget, 18, 19
    continuous monitoring, 20, 21
    costing model,
      identification, 16, 17
    scaling, 19, 20
    size of resources, 17, 18
  monitoring
    Azure Advisor, 34
    Azure cloud cost
      management, 33, 34
  phases, 26
  TCO calculator
    on-premises workloads, 26
    redundancy and license
      requirements, 28
    reports, 29, 30
    server details, 27
    storage and
      networking, 27, 28
  trade-offs, 36, 37
Cybercriminals, 106

D

Data transfer objects (DTOs), 70
Decision-making process, 19
Denial of service (DDoS), 109
Deployment frequency (DF), 40
DevOps model, 40

Digital transformation, 2, 3
Docker-based development
    environments, 43

E

Ecommerce, 10, 11, 21, 22
Everything as code approach
  configuration drifts, 49
  environments, 49
  IAC, 48
  infrastructure deployment/
    updates, 48
  integrating security, 49
  untracked changes, 48

F

Fail fast approach, 7
Failure mode analysis (FMA), 88–89
Financial-sector organizations, 12, 99

G

Georedundant storage (GRS), 18

H, I

Health and life sciences, 10
Hybrid cloud adoption
    methodologies, 2

J

Just-in-time (JIT), 126

K

Kubernetes clusters, 43

L

Line-of-business (LOB), 12, 99
Load testing, 76

M

Mean lead time (MLT), 40
Mean time between failures
    (MTBF), 87
Mean time to recover (MTTR), 41
Microservices-based
    architectures, 11, 12
Microsoft Trust Center, 3
Minimum viable product (MVP), 7
Multiregion testing, 77

N

Network Security Group (NSG), 106
Network Virtual Appliance
    (NVA), 106

O

Open source technologies, 2
Operational excellence
    activity logs, 56, 57
    AKS, 58
    application insights, 53, 54
    application lifecycle, 44

Azure Architecture Center, 59
Azure Monitor, 54, 55
Azure Security Center, 57, 58
considerations, 60, 61
container insights, 56
continuous integration, 45
deployments and rollbacks, 47
design principles
    DevOps, 40, 41
    incidents and failures, 42
    loosely coupled
        applications, 42
    monitoring, 41
    workloads, 41
development environment, 43
elements, 43
everything as code approach,
    48–50
microservices-based
    architectures, 58, 59
monitoring, 53
performance, 50, 51
release performance, 46, 47
source control management, 44
testing, 51, 52
test strategy, 45, 46

P, Q

Peak load testing, 96
Performance efficiency
    design process
        application, 68
        data, 68–70

Performance efficiency (*cont.*)
    infrastructure, 70, 71
    workflow, 67
  Ecommerce, 79
    considerations, 79–82
    web app architecture, 79, 80
  metrics, 63, 64
  monitoring, 77, 78
  performance testing
    considerations, 75
    load testing, 76
    multiregion testing, 77
    nonfunctional aspects, 74
    stress testing, 76
    tools, 74
    user experience, 74
  principles
    anti-patterns, 64, 65
    continuous monitoring/
      optimization, 67
    cost performance balance, 66
    parameters, 64
    peak performance
      capacity, 66
  scalability
    autoscaling, 73
    Azure App Services, 74
    future capacity
      requirements, 71
    scaling up/scaling out, 72
    unit of scale, 72
    VMSS, 73
Personally identifiable information
  (PII), 10, 127

R

Recovery point objective (RPO), 84
Recovery time objective (RTO), 84
Resiliency
  adoption strategies
    dependency management, 94
    managing failures, 93, 94
    regional considerations, 93
  application reliability, 101–103
  availability/recovery target, 86
  design principles
    application/data/
      infrastructure, 84
    automated recovery
      mechanism, 85
    availability targets, 84
    continuous monitoring/
      optimization, 86
    lifecycle management, 85
    performance, 84
    security risks, 85
  financial-sector organizations,
    99, 100
  FMA, 88, 89
  monitoring, 97, 98
  SLAs, 87
  software-as-a-service
    architecture, 100, 101
  test strategies
    backup and DR testing, 96, 97
    best practices, 95
    chaos engineering, 95, 96
    peak load testing, 96

Return on investment (ROI), 15, 106
Robust architecture framework, 5
Role-based access
    control (RBAC), 111

S

Security
    application security, 117, 118
    aspects, 105
    Azure Defender, 126
    Azure Sentinel
        events, 125
        Hunting queries, 126
        overview, 124, 125
        single-stop solution, 124
    cybercriminals, 106
    data protection, 116, 117
    design principles
        CIA, 109
        layers, 109–111
    health and life sciences
        application security, 128, 129
        architecture, 127
        considerations, 127
    identity, 118, 119
    infrastructure segmentation,
        114, 115
    network segmentation, 115, 116
    Security Center
        Azure Security Benchmark,
        120, 121
        comprehensive security, 120
        controls/action, 121, 122

        endpoint threat
          protection, 122
        fusion kill-chain analysis,
          122, 123
        mitigation, 123, 124
        sample alerts, 123
        secure score, 121
        security posture, 120
        workloads, protection, 119
    security intelligence reports, 106
    security pillar
        attackers perspective, 112
        monitoring/optimization, 113
        primary/secondary security
          control, 113
        strategy, 112
        tools/configurations, 112
        zero trust, 113
    shared responsibility model,
        107, 108
    threat vectors
        configuration drifts, 107
        data thefts, 107
        identity breaches, 106
        known vulnerabilities, 107
        malware attacks, 106
        unprotected perimeter, 106
Security information event
    management (SIEM), 124
Security Operations Center
    (SOC), 119
Security orchestration automated
    response (SOAR), 124
Service level agreements (SLAs), 87

Service-level objectives (SLOs),
        64, 84
Shift-left approach, 51, 52
Stress testing, 76

T, U

TCO calculator
    on-premises workloads, 26
    redundancy and license
        requirements, 28
    reports, 29, 30

server details, 27
storage and networking, 27, 28

V

Virtual Machine Scale
        Sets (VMSS), 73
Virtual Network (VNet), 115

W, X, Y, Z

Windows licenses and
        technologies, 2

Printed in the United States
by Baker & Taylor Publisher Services